Also by Robin Noble

Castles in the Mist
North and West

Sagas of
Salt and Stone

Orkney Unwrapped

Robin Noble

Saraband

Published by Saraband
Suite 202, 98 Woodlands Road,
Glasgow, G3 6HB

and

Digital World Centre, 1 Lowry Plaza
The Quays, Salford, M50 3UB
www.saraband.net

10 9 8 7 6 5 4 3 2 1

ISBN: 9781912235025
ISBNe: 9781912235216

Printed and bound in Great Britain by Clays Ltd, St Ives plc.

Descriptions of sites, paths and walking trips do not imply that access is
permitted, nor that these are safe places for inexperienced visitors, in
terms of terrain, weather conditions, tides and other hazards.
Always check before travel whether visits are permitted and/or safe.
No responsibility for safety can be assumed by the author or publisher.

Contents

Map of Orkney

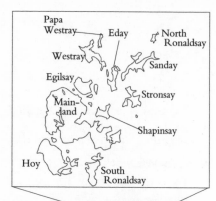

The larger Orkney Islands

Papa Westray
Eday
North Ronaldsay
Westray
Sanday
Egilsay
Stronsay
Main-land
Shapinsay
Hoy
South Ronaldsay

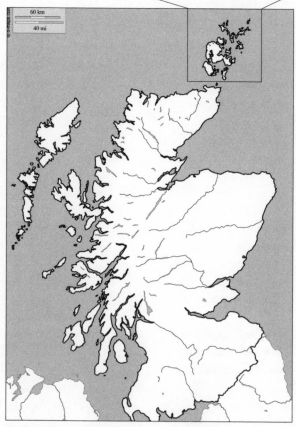

60 km
40 mi

Scale and locator map

For my girls:

*Mairi and Sunni, who shared the happy years in Orkney,
and Sophie, who arrived in our last year there.*

On Places of Power

The Orkney landscape evokes the past as powerfully as that of Greece. I feel this most at the Broch of Gurness, where, on a fine summer day, the shallow, sandy Sound of Eynhallow achieves a brilliance and depth of colour to rival the Mediterranean. And in Orkney a lovely flower, the Grass of Parnassus, makes another Greek connection. But here it grows, as it does not on Mount Parnassus, alongside the tiny, vivid primrose, the *Primula scotica*.

The broch evokes power and heroic exploit, and its circularity, emphasised by ramparts, is a strong element in the landscape. But whereas in Greece so much is history, known and named, here it is all prehistory, unwritten, the builders unnamed, like the robed figures who process across the Birsay stone. They are as enigmatic and as potent as the swirling designs on the lead disc found nearby. Birds fly overhead, a constant and living presence.

Foreword

There is a saying in our household, 'Another first for Papay,' which means any new record-breaking event. It arose from the fact that the small island of Papay found itself in *The Guinness Book of Records* for the shortest commercial flight in the world, 47 seconds from Westray to Papay (Papa Westray), set by Loganair. That was followed by the excavation of Knap of Howar and the discovery from radio-carbon dating that these two stone-built houses are the earliest standing houses in northwestern Europe. Orkney is that kind of place. Quietly spectacular. This is what Robin Noble has captured in his book, with a deep appreciation of Orkney's landscape and history that comes of having lived and worked there. I first came across Robin when he was running the Orkney Field and Arts Centre in Birsay in the northwest corner of Mainland Orkney in the early 1980s, taking small groups of people on walking tours, and it seemed to me that his deep interest in the Orcadian landscape was infectious. So it is in this book, whether he is writing about archaeology and history or birds and wildflowers, and along the way he poses many interesting questions about current ideas and assumptions. He is lucky enough to have family links with Orkney, which adds another dimension to the story.

You will feel after reading this book that you too have explored Orkney with one of Robin's groups, privileged to see the Orkney landscape through his eyes and with his understanding.

Anna Ritchie, Edinburgh

Introduction

When I was young, the road to adventure ran northwards. We called the A9 (wrongly, I think) the Great North Road and thought that we joined it once we reached the Baiglie Straight. This was the best section of the notorious highway, just north of the twisty miles through Glenfarg. Now, I think that we did not reach the A9 itself until we got to Perth, but none of this mattered; we were on our way North.

From as early as I can remember I was entranced by car travel. I spent entire journeys looking out of the side window from the back seat of whichever car we possessed at the time. I vividly recall the dreams that resulted from this particular journey, endless processions of roadside trees, or infinite vistas of moorland and hills as we progressed, sometimes slowly, up the often caravan-clogged road.

In the early days, when the whole family plus luggage fitted into one car, there was actually not much room, and the adults must have blessed the rapt attention I gave to the landscape outside. My parents would sit in the front, with a dog at the feet of whichever of them was not driving. The back seat was occupied by myself and my younger brother, my Highland grandmother who lived with us, her dog, and two cats in boxes. Restless children would not have been popular on these slow journeys from our home in Fife – first of all to a wooden cottage above Loch Ness, and later, to a stone one in a deep, wooded glen in remote Assynt on the West Coast.

My grandmother had known the Highlands all her life, and parts of her inevitable commentary on the route stayed with me in my sleep. It was the hypnotic procession of river names that beguiled my dreams, and they remain evocative for me to this day. The majestic Tay, half-seen Tummel, the sadly depleted Garry, the infant Truim then the upland Spey, the Findhorn with its croys and astonishingly ugly bridge, the serenity of the Ness as it flowed through Inverness, Capital of the Highlands. The latter river we crossed by a narrow bridge with more than a touch of the Scots Baronial about it.

Often we stopped away from the main road, turning right just after the Bogroy Inn, lunching and quickly walking the dogs in the nearby forest, before joining the highway again just before the arched bridge over the River Beauly. The old A9 wended its way around the firths, so we next crossed the Conon before passing through Dingwall and along the shore of the Cromarty Firth. We then headed over Struie Hill, crossing the river now called the Alness but which has an older, more interesting name, the Averon, gaining Bonar Bridge before turning westwards up the long reach of the Kyle of Sutherland into which flows the Shin. Each name would be said out loud, each ritual utterance signifying a further step in the right direction. We followed the Oykell (joined by the Cassley) towards the isolated, monumental hills of Coigach and Assynt, and, now rather running out of rivers, it was their names that led us to our destination, Glenleraig. There we would spend the enchanted weeks of those long-ago summer holidays.

There were other, magical names that we sometimes followed yet farther north: the dark waters of the Laxford, and the Dionard, which led to the incredible beauty of Durness and Balnakiel. This was the beginning, as far as we were concerned, of the North Coast, which possessed a romance of its own, being the extreme northern limit of the mainland of Great Britain. But we knew, almost from infancy, however vaguely, that there was land still farther to the north. We saw it once in those early years (I must have been about nine or ten, my brother more than two years younger) when our grandmother took us for a week's holiday to Tongue. From some headland reaching far out into the sea, we glimpsed dim, gentle shapes, the Islands of Orkney, with which, we gathered (at that time, even more vaguely!) we had many connections.

During the succeeding years, the extent of our involvement with Orkney began to come clearer, and that distant archipelago started to lay its own claims on me. In Assynt, partly through the enthusiasm of my grandmother, archaeology had become one of my passions. Two locations in particular had fired this enthusiasm: the splendid chaos of the Broch of Clachtoll and the mysterious and wonderful Bone Caves in a narrow glen near Inchnadamph. Then my grandmother gave me a book on archaeology, which I read and reread. I still have it. It is entitled, almost baldly, *The Northern Isles*, edited by F.T. Wainwright. That simple present had far-reaching consequences. It did far more than establish my enthusiasm for ancient peoples and the structures they built – it played a major role in shaping the future path of my life.

As soon as I could drive I went in the little car I had inherited from a great-aunt (and in which, importantly, I could sleep) to Orkney on a voyage of adventure and discovery. I know, of course, that nowadays boys and girls of the same age trek through Nepal, or walk the length of South America. I am full of admiration for them, but I was not particularly enterprising or adventurous, and I was determined to explore the riches of my homeland. My focus was mainly on the archaeological riches of Mainland Orkney, but along with them I drank in much more, and from then on, Orkney's presence lurked somewhere at the back of my mind as a place to which I would return.

And so, about a dozen years later, I did. I was married then, with two small daughters. We had been living in Assynt (not far from Inchnadamph, in that same limestone corridor) when the idea of spreading our wings a bit began to appeal. We got hold of the particulars of something called the "Orkney Field and Arts Centre". There were a few pictures of a grey sandstone house against an endless sea, under a huge sky, and it appeared that we could make of it precisely what we wanted. With a confidence that now takes my breath away, we decided to do exactly that, and my life as an interpreter of landscape, an explainer of almost anything from the rocks upward, began. Of one thing at least I soon had no doubt: the natural world, with all its beauty and complex connections, would be my focus for the rest of my life. Archaeology was not only inspiring in itself, but by studying past cultures, we could work out aspects of the world they had lived in, which had shaped them, and which they had influenced, and which, ultimately, went to make the environment in which we live today.

At a more immediate level I learned more about my family's connections with these islands. It turned out that the farm surrounding our base in Birsay, at the northwest corner of Mainland Orkney, had once been owned by one of my ancestors, a woman whose story was fascinating in its own right. Every generation since, even after my great-great-grandmother had left Orkney, had returned there, for far more than simple holidays. Even as the power of Orkney over my mind slowly grew, I learned more of the significance it held for earlier members of my family. And once I was established and working there, I could see how its entrancing and enduring aspects impressed countless members of the public over the following decades.

This book explores these aspects, those effects. It makes no attempt to be anything but personal, but it is the result of forty-seven years of visits, looking and thinking, wondering and asking (and answering!) a multitude of questions. I have always felt, when in Orkney, that I belong there, that I am at home there, and this is, if you like, my thanks to the islands themselves, and, above all, to their wonderful people.

One

The Look of the Land

Around the middle of October 2015, I returned to Orkney for a few days. It was at this same time of year, thirty-five years earlier, that I had completed my very first season teaching at the Orkney Field and Arts Centre. It was even longer, forty-seven years, since I had first come to Orkney "under my own steam", and this most recent arrival bore no resemblance to any visits during the intervening years. For a start, it was dark, simply because of what I still regard as a very complex ferry timetable. The truth is that it merely reflects today's greatly increased traffic, but it still felt very strange to pass the cliffs of Hoy and see nothing. The entry into the ferry was as different from that first trip as it could be, too. Now I drove along the ramp into the cavernous and almost empty interior of a big, modern ship; then, I vividly recall standing on the quayside as my precious little car was lifted into the air and swung over till it was above the hold, before being slowly let down into a tight space between other vehicles. Time has marched on, ferries have changed. The question at the back of my mind was how much Orkney might also have changed without me noticing it.

I drove the road from Stromness to Kirkwall in the dark, still feeling rather strange, and was glad of the familiar, warm welcome at my accommodation. I slept well, too, and caught up with family news over a hearty breakfast. Feeling rather more as if I belonged now, I set off to look around the West Mainland on a remarkably calm morning. As I drove that familiar main road – unchanged, I think, in all the years I have known it – past the big farm of Quanterness, I began to notice that ahead of me the clouds were thinning. Light began to dapple the water of Wide Firth and, before long, I decided I had to stop to photograph the scene. So, roughly below the Old Manse of Firth (where Jo Grimond, former leader of the Liberal Party and something of a power in the land, once lived), I parked the car and waited till the traffic would let me cross.

It was autumn, and all the tall roadside grass and meadowsweet was straw-coloured and dull brown. The tide was lowish, and the sea-weed's ochre was bright – the strongest visible colour. The smooth, flowing shape of the far shore, the hill-ridge that forms the rim of the basin of the West Mainland, was a smooth progression of almost pastel shades, mostly assorted greens and fawns, with the deep brown of heather. The whole was dotted with the white of houses, and, above, the subtlest sky imaginable, pearlescent, all reflected perfectly in the still sea. The overall effect was timeless, magical.

For many, this Orkney landscape tends to be described in nega-tive terms. It is "not very hilly", or "almost devoid of trees", or "just mostly farmland" – statements I have often heard. Such comments have the contradictory capacity to be almost true while at the same time being almost totally untrue. One thing is definitely true: this terrain offers a complete contrast to the dramatic landscape of Assynt, which we had left to move to the islands. In general, Orkney has subtler attractions – apart, that is, from the great sea-cliffs. It is a land of smooth, flowing shapes, embellished by the geometric patterns of fields in their infinite variety of greens, punctuated by the fluid shapes of lochs or inlets, reflecting the huge sky above. A "designer's landscape", I often thought, inspiration for many artists and craftsmen. It is no surprise to me that one of the many Orcadian jewellers has achieved success with her enamels.

This smooth landscape derives from a relatively simple geology. Most of what you see consists of one rock type, known as Old Red Sandstone. As it happens, it is not particularly old, being roughly 400 million years in age, nor is it always red, so this information is not as helpful as you might at first think. This sandstone rests on a basement of older rock, which appears on the surface in a very small area, from the hills south of Yesnaby, via Stromness, to the coast of the Island of Graemsay. Here some metamorphic rocks, schist and gneiss are visible, as well as some granite. These rocks lack the obvious structure of the sandstone and give rise to a more acid soil, but their most obvious legacy, in Orcadian terms, is that they include Brinkie's Brae, the relatively steep and conspicuous hill immediately behind Stromness.

The Old Red Sandstone is a sedimentary rock laid down in a wide lake basin that was part of a large depression to the east and north of the Scottish Highlands. Then, as now, long rivers brought eroded sediments from the mountain chain into the alluvial basin that roughly corresponds with the area we now call the Moray Firth, and into a freshwater lake farther north that has been christened Lake Orcadie. The lake levels fluctuated as the rainfall increased and decreased, and the accumulated sediments assumed different colours according to their depth and composition. The red that gives the whole formation its name is from the sediments of the lake margins. At times the muddy sediment will have dried out, which results in stones with mud-cracking, while others reflect the ripple marks of sandy shores.

Later, dense deposits of sand and gravel covered the dried-up lake, but these sediments, even when consolidated through the immense ages of geological time, remained relatively soft, porous and easily eroded. The generally subdued relief of Orkney's hills reflects the erosion of successive Ice Ages; differential resistance to this erosion in various layers of sandstone can be seen in the bands of crags on the Island of Hoy and in the terrace formations on Rousay. Since the last glaciation, the main cause of erosion has been wind and sea. This has given rise to the dramatic coastal formations within the archipelago. Erosion has of course produced spectacular cliffs, particularly in the West Mainland and in Hoy, but the deposition of the eroded sediment has had other effects. As well as extending islands such as Sanday, it has joined many former islands – for instance, Deerness – to the adjoining Mainland or to other islands. The process has also blocked several inlets with storm beaches, and provided us with many beautiful expanses of sand.

Talk of erosion has taken us past the formation of the third main rock type to be seen within Orkney: the volcanic. At various periods, cracks have appeared in the matrix sandstone, through which rock from the earth's molten core has risen up. Evidence of this is sometimes seen around the coast, where cracks at 90 degrees to the matrix rock are known as volcanic dykes. A conspicuous example cuts through the flagstone of the beach at the very tip of the Point of Buckquoy in Birsay. And the Old Man of Hoy sits on a platform of lava, and the dark blue boulders, which contrast so wonderfully with the pink sandstone on Rackwick's lovely shore, derive from a volcanic sill, seen in the cliffs to the north side of that bay.

Two aspects of the sandstone that forms the archipelago make it particularly attractive. One is that the sediments were laid down in horizontal layers, or strata, that have remained largely undisturbed. They are of varying thicknesses, and in some places can be quite easily persuaded, whether by the sea or by man, to separate into their distinct bands – some thin enough for roofing, some thick enough for building-blocks. In addition, when they crack naturally in the horizontal plane, they tend to do so in straight lines. Thus, many shores are embellished by geometric shapes, parallelograms, even triangles, such as would delight the heart of any builder. This makes it relatively simple to quarry, but, at the same time, therein lies the main problem for the builder, whether of broch or 1913 guest-house (the origin of our home). Once used, the sandstone will often continue to split, causing at worst slumping, or, at best, easy ingress of water. This is why so many old stone houses in Orkney, as in Stromness, for instance, are harled. However, this is a minor disadvantage (unless you are faced with a wet gable!) when compared to the other characteristics that make it such a wonderful building stone, responsible for all the marvellous structures from prehistory and history that make Orkney a special place.

The other critical aspect is the fertile nature of this rock, blessed as it is with minerals from long-eroded mountains and organic matter from the lakes from which it originated. The appearance of the islands on a bright summer day, rich and green and yet so far north, immediately highlights the importance of geology. It is not the rain that makes the landscape so green, but the soil that derives from the underlying rock.

It is the prosperity that has come from this underlying fertility, and given rise to the wonderful buildings of almost every period, that makes Orkney so remarkable. This is not to imply that Orkney has always, and for everyone, been a prosperous place. There are, of course, areas of poor ground, and have been years (or decades, or centuries) of poor weather.

What Orkney does share with other northern areas (although here it has been significantly reduced over the ages) is a covering of peat. Despite the porous nature of the sandstone, and the islands' modest rainfall, the low summer temperatures in these northern latitudes ensure that most of the rain that falls remains in the ground. And as the ground is on an almost level base in many places, there is a tendency for it to become waterlogged, favouring the formation of peat. This was for a very long time important as a domestic fuel, and many hill areas still show the dark lines of old peat banks. The difficulty of draining level areas of peat basin or wetland means that older farms tend to be located on gently sloping ground with reasonable drainage. Later, heavy machinery enabled the draining of these flat zones, and allowed the hills to be reclaimed. The conversion of heather to grass began in earnest in the Victorian period and continued until grants for such work had ceased. It had virtually stopped by the 1980s when we were living there.

While some may dislike the visible results of this period of reclamation – the geometric shapes of green against the dark heather of the unreclaimed land – our landscape remains an attractive mosaic of farmland, wetland and hill. With all three categories in abundance, wildlife may wander comparatively unmolested through diverse botanical reserves. Orkney is far more than "just mostly farmland", and the large bodies of freshwater within that farmland are as important to the landscape and the wildlife as they are to the fisherman.

If you have to fly in to the islands (which, in poetic theory at least, should be reached by boat), you will get an excellent view of the jigsaw puzzle of land and water that makes up the archipelago. Unlike Shetland to the north, which has a sensible, linear feel, Orkney from the air spreads in all directions. Westray is heading for Labrador, North Ronaldsay for Norway, South Ronaldsay content to feel its easier way to Caithness. But once you have landed, it is given a more unified feel by the protective presence of the Hoy hills, which hide the southern island of Great Britain and emphasise our need for mental self-sufficiency.

It is surprisingly easy to be urban in outlook in Orkney, to be unaware of the sea at times, although for many it is a constant presence. When I was living in Birsay, I was conscious of a vast and brilliant light to the West, the sun in our enormous open sky flaring off the ocean, which lapped (at times!) against the angled slabs of our lovely bay. But everyone is dominated by the weather that comes off that surrounding sea, and after days of wind everything feels and tastes of salt. The northern, oceanic weather is a reality that at times beggars belief. Once, in the short days near Christmas, I had to take the car out in a major gale. When coming home around the very northwest corner of the Mainland, past Costa Head and Swannay Farm, I reached a point from which there can be a sublime view of the Brough of Birsay with its lighthouse, and the cliffs of Marwick Head, crowned by the Kitchener Memorial. Today, there was no glorious shining sea. A ferocious band of towering waves was pounding the cliffs and the beach, wild water backed up to the West appearing higher than our little, low village, and I began to wonder whether we really could survive the night.

Wind may seem a constant in the islands, and it is certainly very hard to find shelter from it, but I remember a day (part of an astounding week) when with friends and family, scantily clad, we lay in the hot sun on the wide, opalescent sand-bars of Waulkmill Bay. The turquoise water barely lifted, even as the tide rose around us. My records suggest that the weather actually was better then; the late springs and early summers were certainly much warmer, and there was more drying weather. Ponds, which did not exist in the years I lived there, have slowly appeared over the intervening decades. While early human inhabitants, growing their own crops where those fields are now, will no doubt have helped to clear the ground of tall vegetation, the salt-laden winds have done at least as much, and it is very difficult to re-establish bushes where no shelter exists. The wind does not affect only the trees (or what might become trees were they growing elsewhere). I was once walking south of Yesnaby, over the short heather moorland there, when a

7

visitor, a very competent naturalist, pointed out the effects of fire in the heather. I had to tell him, very gently, that he was wrong; it was the effect of endless, salt-laden gales. Apart from shaping the coast-line itself, and the vegetation of the islands, these storms impose some sort of discipline on the lives of those who have to cope with them; anything left outside may simply disappear overnight if the wind gets up. It often occurred to me that the havoc of Mischief Night (Hallowe'en elsewhere), when gangs of kids roamed around, moving anything transportable and leaving it to be found in the morning in as awkward and public a place as possible, was really part of the necessary preparation for the regular gales of winter.

Two

Days on Marwick Head

"Even before I left my home on the edge of the small village of The Palace (named after the ruins of the elegant summer residence of the first Stewart Earl of Orkney), it was obvious that it was going to be a special day. A few companions and I were starting to walk over the short, flowery turf of the Links (machair, it would be in the Western Isles) to the edge of Birsay Bay. It was already warm, promising to be significantly hot, perhaps, but the day seemed, in matters meteorological, to be somewhat complex.

Despite the warmth, there was a stiff breeze from the sea and, as we began the gentle ascent of the long, slow incline that leads up to the top of the cliffs of Marwick Head, we could see below us, in the shadow under the cliff edge, a narrow band of thick mist. In the strong breeze, this mist continually boiled up to, and over, the cliff edge, only to disappear almost immediately in the heat of the already brilliant sun. Slowly it thinned, but the effect, as we gained height, of the bright light on our left, and the fog on our right, was of strange unreality.

These first cliffs are principally the haunt of shag and fulmar, whose guttural conversations below us seemed fiendishly magnified by these conditions. Occasionally a bird would emerge dramatically out of the fog, sometimes really close to us, and, seeming equally disoriented by the unusual weather, would hastily retreat with a loud squawk. All the while, a few yards away on our left, the calm and beautiful cows of Orkney grazed placidly on the rich grass.

As we walked further, the mist thinned and the sounds of birdlife below us increased. There was a steady fly-past, nearly always it seemed from north to south, of those impressive – if not always likeable – birds, the greater black-backed gulls and the great skuas (or bonxies as they are known). Small flotillas of rapidly flapping torpedo-shaped auks hurtled past, and as we gained the level heights of the headland and turned to face the shallow, cliff-girt bay, a truly spectacular sight met our eyes.

Nothing can match the excitement, the noise, even the smell of a major seabird colony in June. Thousands of birds lined the ledges of the vertical sandstone cliff, while equal numbers appeared ceaselessly engaged in flying in and out of invisible holes in the rock face, or crash-landing in non-existent gaps in the serried ranks of their fellows. And down there, through the fast-thinning fog, where the great rollers crashed white, were yet more birds – razorbills, guillemots, puffins, kittiwakes and fulmars, merest dots on the water far below us. I have a favourite vantage point, a small amphitheatre set at an angle to the main cliff, which provides the perfect view along the rock face to the tower of the Kitchener Memorial, and there we lay in safety at the cliff edge, drinking in the whole scene. Orkney's brilliant light blazed overhead, the vibrant colours of sea and grass, of the drifts of sea campion and thrift at the rock margin, and of the myriad, cascading birds completely filled our senses. It was hard to drag ourselves away, as eventually we did.

We wandered along the headland, under the tower, and began the gentle descent to the southern bay, which is Marwick "proper" (wick or vik meaning a bay or harbour). The view from here southwards is over the smooth, flowing land of the West Mainland to the higher bulk of Hoy, with the chimney-stack feature of the famed Old Man. The day was now brilliantly clear, and the whole line of the north coast of Scotland could easily be seen, with all its ranked hills – the Griams, Clibreck,

Loyal (looking much more impressive than it does from the south), Hope and the Cape Wrath hills, even the grey ridges of Foinaven.

Marwick itself is now useless as a harbour, even as a place to pull a boat up on the shore, as it is blocked by a storm beach of large boulders. The enclosed lagoon provides a nice area of sheltered water where once, descending from the high cliffs, I saw an otter swimming. Today we were not so lucky, but there were two shelduck dames with their crèche of youngsters, some eider duck and the inevitable, noisy oystercatchers. Farther to the south, in contrast to the lofty cliffs now left behind, the shore is low and level, at the most perhaps fifteen feet above the expanse of canted slabs, which are all that protect it from the might of the Atlantic. Despite this apparent lack of shelter, this section of the coast is not bare or eroded by the storms of winter as are other parts; on the contrary, it is well-vegetated, the pale blue of spring squill now giving place to the thrift.

Eventually one comes to one of my favourite places, the inlet of Sand Geo with its beautifully built drystone fishermen's huts and their nousts (boat-shaped depressions into which small boats were pulled to avoid being smashed in the winter tempests). From the huts there is a short, steepish descent to the beach of grey boulders, below which there is a little sand and some deep and beautiful rock pools. The water in these is as clear as crystal, the weeds in them many and various, coloured brilliant green, red or dark brown, and their rocky sides have a cream-to-purple encrustation that can appear sky-blue in some lights. Here we sat, or wandered and pottered about, or dozed in the warmth. It is always a comfortable place.

After a while we enjoyed a cup of thermos tea and a discussion about the flagstones that form the roof of the huts — they could so obviously just have been lifted from the nearby beach — then we slowly retraced our steps. It was now late afternoon, but the sun behind us was as bright and warm as at midday and, rather strangely, we were apparently the only people about.

And as we walked along quietly, from the shining ocean on our left there leaped a pair of dolphins (we later decided after a lot of discussion that they were white-sided dolphins). As we strolled, so they swam on a parallel course along the shore, regularly breaching, silhouetted against the flood of light. After the initial excitement, we became quiet, full of wonder at the beauty of the spectacle, and my friends, who were older than I and less inclined to walk as fast, asked if I would like to go on at my own pace.

And so I walked alone, along that magical shore, over the cliffs of the headland, pausing at the corner from where my old grey home could be seen, and where later, grass of Parnassus, a flower of great significance for me, would bloom. Behind me, the clamour of the bird cliffs, on my left the endless ocean. As I turned to scan the horizon, two streamlined shapes leaped once again from the depths, sending light cascading.

All the beauty of nature, all of the richness and fecundity of the Orkney summer, was fixed for me in that wonderful moment. Such memories sustain us through the grey and wind of winter."

The above account was written for my first generally published book, *North and West*, which appeared in 2003. Since then, I have walked that same route a number of times, and have been along the cliff-top of Marwick on countless occasions. Inevitably, through the intervening years, some things have changed, or my perceptions of them have altered.

Marwick Head is still a most beautiful and impressive place, and there are still lots of birds to be seen, despite considerable reductions in most species. This is especially true of the kittiwake, a bird whose numbers seem to be prone to wide fluctuations over time. The reduction may be due to factors such as over-fishing of sand eels, or climatic change warming the waters off Orkney, altering the levels at which the sand eels now swim and making them inaccessible to the birds. I certainly miss the great contribution their flocks used to make to the excitement of the early summer. A thousand birds at a time might gather on the extensive rocks of Birsay Bay at low tide. They would suddenly take off, calling loudly, and fly together over our house to the freshwater of Boardhouse Loch, where the whole crowd bathed and splashed. Other seabirds are doing better, and the Noup Head gannetry in Westray has been growing rather than declining. I defy anyone to describe accurately the extraordinary noise of a gannetry at its height, and on a visit to Marwick Head in 2015 I was delighted to see a number of gannets at one corner of the cliffs. If this new colony (I am fairly sure some birds were attempting to breed) is successful, then it will definitely add to the attractions of this wonderful location.

The place where we used to lie down and look along the cliff remains a fine viewpoint, but in the intervening years I have looked very carefully at its shape and have decided that I was wrong to think that it could be natural. It must in fact be man-made, and a quarry – one, moreover, from which substantial stones were taken. This could have been done at any stage in history, of course, but the largest stones, those one might properly call megaliths, could have been used in the erection of the great stone circles and associated buildings such as Maeshowe, the finest of all the chambered tombs. The source of the stone for these great monuments has been of interest for some considerable time, and I like the thought that some of the amazing sandstone slabs that make up Maeshowe, for instance, might just have come from one of the most dramatic locations on our coast.

Marwick Head is crowned by the stark, battlemented tower that is by custom called the Kitchener Memorial. It was apparently raised precisely to be that, and I have always been unhappy that it commemorates the death of one single man, however notable in our national

13

history he may have been. It is now estimated that 737 men died when HMS *Hampshire* hit a mine off Marwick in June 1916 and sank. The story may be too well known to need repeating here, but there are a number of mysteries concerning the events and responses to it that are worth considering. Lord Kitchener, then Minister of War, was apparently on an urgent mission to meet the Czar of Russia. It is surprising that a man with such enormous responsibilities at a time of war could actually be spared to make that long voyage, which would have been around the North Cape of Norway, a distance that would have taken weeks, surely, rather than days. The initial response to the sinking by those in charge of local defence matters appears to have been strange: men from nearby Birsay and Marwick (presumably using the fishermen's huts) were forbidden to take out boats to see if they could pick up survivors, to me an extraordinary and callous decision.

Another anomaly came to light only when we were living there. One day, a substantial vessel, a bit like an oil-rig supply boat, arrived and anchored in the middle of the bay, between the headland and the tidal Brough of Birsay. Through the binoculars we could see quite a lot of activity, despite the distance, and the older locals confirmed that she was anchored above the wreck of the *Hampshire*. We established that divers were going down, and after a while that objects were being recovered from the seabed. For quite some time, there appeared to be no official reaction, and the process continued. During this period it emerged that, incomprehensibly, the *Hampshire* had never been declared a War Grave, despite the enormous loss of life. It was, therefore, not clear on what legal grounds the activity could be stopped. Eventually, it was halted and several of the objects recovered were taken into official custody; they included the huge propeller, which may be seen at the museum at Lyness on Hoy. And, to our great relief, the ship was at last declared a War Grave.

It has, however, taken until now for the final omission to be rectified; a memorial wall being constructed around the tower so that those who perished with Kitchener will at last receive the recognition they have so long deserved. I am glad now to have seen it completed.

In my original account, I used the word "oyce" in connection with the tidal lagoon of Marwick, which was created by the formation of the storm beach. This is a name you may see in print, or on maps, but rarely hear. Because I had an innate doubt about it, I asked a young Orcadian friend what he thought the origin of the word might be. The spelling I automatically discounted, assuming that it is one of those romantic Victorian effusions that tend to distort our language in particular contexts: "ye olde englishe fyne fayre", that sort of thing. True enough, the word an Orcadian would use, my friend said, is pronounced something like "euss", where the "eu" is as in the French "deux" or "Meuse". It is obviously connected to Ouse, that English river name meaning slow or still water, which must also be of Scandinavian origin. (Thanks, Colin!) The storm beach itself is called an ayre, a name you will see around the islands, but presumably once again with an over-fancy spelling.

There are fewer eider in Marwick or generally around these coasts now, and markedly fewer shelduck, and I remain unconvinced that this decline is being taken adequately seriously. I find this worrying, and feel that the late Ian Prestt of the RSPB would have disapproved. He was very keen on "holding the line", maintaining that all the local populations of various species of bird are important. This was based on the very simple and obvious logic that all these small local populations make up the national populations, the headline figures that concern us all. The reduction in the numbers of these ducks puzzles me somewhat, as the places where they feed, such as Birsay Bay or the Sound of Eynhallow, seem unaltered, unharmed by development of any kind. The places where the eiders nest may well be subject to more human disturbance, but shelduck take over rabbit burrows, and those remain viable homes for them long after any rabbits may have disappeared for whatever reason.

Sand Geo, with its huts apparently growing out of the bedrock, has always been a favourite destination, and when eventually we decided to leave Orkney for pastures new, it was one of the places to which we made a special pilgrimage. The beach I have simply described as being of grey stones, which is true, but not enough. Many of the stones have fascinating patterns, some the relics of ancient mud-crackings, some the ripples from much older shores, some just the result of erosion through time. They are very beautiful, and the rock pools, as I said, are lovely. While my wife sat on the short grass with the new baby, my second daughter examined the patterns on the stones, and the eldest looked into the still pools. I took a photograph, which I still have. It is very special, and for more reasons than I then knew.

The great headland remains a wonderful viewpoint, whether south to the heights of Hoy and the hills of the North Coast, or north over the sweep of Birsay Bay to the Brough with the low snout of Rousay beyond and, in the distance, the length of Westray, culminating in the hill and cliffs of Noup Head. To the west is the ever-restless sea, and to the east, the quiet, smooth harmony of the fields of the West Mainland. This landscape is blatantly man-made, a human construct, created by our activity over thousands of years, but none the worse for that. It is a landscape about which you can come to feel passionately, and at the very end of the text of *North and West* I was moved to quote a short poem by Robert Rendall, a fascinating man, whom I sadly never knew, but friends did. I often think of his words when I stand on the crest of Marwick Head:

The solitudes of land and sea assuage
my quenchless thirst for freedom unconfined;
with independent heart and mind
hold I my heritage.

Three

Clothing the Land

Along the shore to the Fishermen's Huts, along the crest of Marwick Head and, in particular, on much of the perimeter of the beautiful tidal island of the Brough of Birsay, a small, blue, lily-like flower grows in great profusion: the spring squill. From our house on the Links, I have seen the southern end of the Brough appear as blue as the sky on a soft summer day, an elusive and transient beauty. Even alongside the shorter track that leads up to the cliff edge from Comloquoy, under the prosaic fences, you may find this tiny, exquisite flower. It grows, too, in places with short grass around the great Ring of Brodgar. My mother who, as a Wren, was stationed in Orkney during the Second World War, remembered taking one of the North Isles ferries in the early summer, passing small islands ("holms" they are called here) and headlands, blue-stained and reflected, shimmering, in the silken sea.

Like the equally tiny endemic, the famous *Primula scotica*, this plant can cope with only the shortest of grass, whether cropped by rabbits or livestock, or heavily suppressed by the wind. Here are plants that are obviously deeply influenced by the weather but also, perhaps, by man's agricultural management, especially the grazing of stock. The profusion of blooming primulas can be manipulated by altering grazing patterns, and it has struck me that there has clearly existed, perhaps for a very long time, some sort of relationship between these plants and the activities of Orkney's farmers.

Although it is hard to judge with any accuracy the ebb and flow of agricultural activity through the ages, the contrasting blocks of green may have been interspersed with almost transparent washes of blue, just as there remain today quite large areas of the thick, creamy-white of meadowsweet, heavy with scent.

This, I think, is one of the constant delights of the Orcadian land-scape. It is not really a place to seek some hugely rare flower; it is a place instead to enjoy common plants growing in a marvellous pro-fusion, an exuberance that, on a winter visit, is hard to credit. The thrift, in all possible shades of pink, which in some years may follow the squill, is one such plant. Bird's-foot trefoil is another, as are the exotic-looking yellow flag irises, or the sturdy angelica that marches along the Marwick shore.

Early man, arriving in a quiet inlet of Scapa Flow such as Waulkmill Bay, (but we know that our islands have long been slowly sinking so where they first trod and settled must now be firmly under the sea) would have marvelled at the exuberance of common plants found elsewhere in the Highlands, as I did on my own arrival from the more acid soils of Assynt. Tormentil, the ubiquitous little yellow-starred creeper of the moorland, or the golden marsh mari-gold of the wet places, both grow on a scale I had not known before, and gladden the heart. The tall crimson spikes of northern marsh orchids enjoy the fertility here, and even the peaty moorlands may be rich with the heath-spotted orchid.

My first solo visit to Orkney was partly because I was inquisi-tive. I wanted to know the reality of these islands about which I had heard and read so much, and as a teenager and fledgling driver, I felt mildly adventurous and wanted to explore on my own. Similar motives may have inspired the first explorers, although it is tanta-lisingly uncertain when they first arrived and how they crossed the Pentland Firth. Orkney had long been separated from the mainland

we now call Scotland; there has never been any suggestion of a helpful land bridge to assist the leap from Caithness, to which Hoy and
South Ronaldsay are temptingly close. However they achieved the
crossing, these early explorers would rapidly have discovered that a
whole country lay before them. In it grew many of the plants they
associated with fertility, such as the dark crimson-flowered marsh
cinquefoil, another plant of the wetlands that covered much more of
the land than they do now. The first explorers must have been hunter-gatherers and these rich, marshy places, alive with wildfowl (such
as the Loons of today) would have been of considerable importance
to them.

The plants, and what they signified, will have meant more perhaps to the first farmers, and as they brought stock with them, and
grew crops, something recognisably like agriculture rapidly began
to modify, in various ways, the landscape of the archipelago. It
amounts to more than simply grazing animals and growing crops.
While we were living in Birsay, a lovely young lad stayed with us
one summer. His name was Ian Simpson, last met as a professor in
Stirling University. He was researching the extent and creation of
"made", in other words, manured, soil in the valley of Marwick.
From his work it has become clear that the Vikings who settled and
farmed there improved the soil, in addition to other agricultural
practices. And it is entirely possible that they were not the first to do
so. Through archaeology we are learning more and more about the
sophisticated techniques of our ancestors, once regarded as primitive. There is a good possibility that their agricultural methods were
also quite intelligent and not based, as there has been a tendency to
think, solely on extracting the goodness from the soil, without care
or husbandry. It seems clear that initially farmers would move into
areas that looked naturally suitable, those that did not need to be
drained or cleared. It's also likely they took up only a small area of

land growing arable crops. As grazing animals would either be tethered as they were in Orkney well into recent times (I recall an old woman living above Boardhouse Loch who tethered calves behind her cottage) or herded, it is also probable that some care was taken not to destroy what patches of woodland had survived the windy climate. They would surely have been too valuable, whether as a source of sticks for lighting fires, or for shelter both for stock and some less hardy plants.

Nevertheless, I am clear that native woodland in Orkney has long been under-estimated. There has always been a little bit more than most people either thought or noticed; the problem was that they were looking too high for it. I am reminded of the joke question: "What do you do if you are lost in an Icelandic forest?" Answer: "Stand up!" Scattered in a number of locations, mostly dampish places, are several groups of extensive "tree-mounds", generally of willow. These may be only six feet high, but they can be many times that in circumference. Individual plants may cover a surprising amount of ground, offering valuable shelter to insects – and the birds that eat them. I think particularly of the stonechat and reed bunting, although in recent years with a succession of cold springs, they have become noticeably more difficult to see. The distinction between trees and shrubs in Orkney is rather meaningless, and the scrub woodland with which people associate the early landscape is more likely to have consisted of "trees" of this shape rather than tall, straight trunks. Goodness knows how old these willow mounds must be, but their presence is a continuation of an ancient and somewhat under-appreciated habitat, as I am positive that no one ever bothered to plant them. They are found, if you start to look for them, in a number of places: the flat ground on either side of the by-road from Norseman Village up to the Chair of Lyde is full of them.

What is always referred to as the "most northerly natural

woodland in Britain", that of Berriedale in Hoy, had, when I used to visit it, other species including downy birch, rowan, hazel and aspen, and it has very slowly expanded since those days. The two principal glens across north Hoy both show quite a lot of regeneration in the past thirty or more years. Progress has been slow, however, perhaps simply due to climatic factors, or perhaps also because of the peaty nature of the soil that covers the underlying sand and alluvium. Within the same period, planting of both native trees and exotics across Orkney has really taken off, and the landscape, for instance of Rendall and the East Mainland, is becoming more diverse. Most people are happy to plant what will grow, whether native or exotic, a pragmatic attitude that does not trouble me much. I appreciate that there are places where the *Rubus* that is often called salmonberry has in recent years become something of a pest – mainly, I think, in areas where there has been less grazing of stock, as in parts of Rousay. But sycamore has shown no tendency to overwhelm Orkney, and its plantations around the big houses such as Binscarth and Balfour are an important part of the landscape and local history. Incidentally, one sycamore in Kirkwall has possibly given rise to much of the misapprehension that Orkney is treeless. I refer to the tree in Broad Street that is rather mysteriously referred to as the "Big Tree" or simply "the Tree", as if it were either the largest, or the only one within the town – or the archipelago! There are several, much larger trees, only a few yards away, between the ruins of the Palaces and the warm sandstone of the cathedral – which look most attractive on a sunny day. Finstown, too, has a pleasant urban and wooded character, which should be explored and appreciated by more people.

It was the Victorians who planted most of the sycamores, and who radically transformed the look of much of Orkney, in a wide-ranging reorganisation of agriculture that gave us the big rectangular fields of today. They drained, ploughed, fertilised and reseeded large areas. Were any of them to return, they would find the look of the land familiar. It is certainly true, though, that the crops and methods of harvesting have significantly changed over subsequent years. Fields of bere (a form of barley), barley itself and oats have become quite rare, and in my time, the amounts of oilseed rape and potatoes appear to have fluctuated significantly too. Where the Orkney farmer really seems to excel is in grassland management. The rate of growth of the grass in spring can be quite remarkable, and presumably is more dependent on daylight hours than actual warmth. In good years, I have seen a field give three crops: two of silage and one of hay. Chemical weedkillers rarely seem to be used, and sheets of dandelions, quite magnificent when in bloom, as well as the less picturesque dockens appear to bear this out, and are certainly good for birds. The characteristic patchwork of different shades of green is the result of varied cutting dates and stages of regrowth, which provides a variety of resources for the birds. Newly cut areas will often be visited by waders as well as the ubiquitous gulls and rooks. The autumn fields still have large flocks of waders. On my October visit, I spent some twenty minutes leaning on a dyke, watching a field occupied by some large, clean, beautiful cows. Around them were perhaps 150 curlews, elegantly working their way over the grass, and between them scurried the same number of golden plover, less spectacular than when in their breeding plumage, but dappled, mottled, intricate in the soft light.

The curlew could be the emblematic bird of Orkney. Its haunting music, which may greet you if you stop the car and open the windows when driving through the Orphir valley of Kirbister in early summer, is an integral part, for me at least, of the magic of the Isles. It is claimed that Orkney has the highest density of breeding curlew in the world, but also that their numbers are declining. It is of course sadly true that numbers of nearly every bird appear, countrywide, to be in decline. But the curlew in Orkney provides some clues as to the reasons, not least because it is so visible on the islands. Predators are usually listed as among the likely causes, but we can confidently say that there are few mammalian predators here: no foxes, badgers, pine martens or wildcats, for instance. As for domestic or feral cats, it would be interesting to know if they have increased in the past few decades, and whether they tend to concentrate on the local rats – which could in turn impact on the bird population by eating eggs. Weasels and stoats were listed as absent, but that has changed. In the past five years, stoats (which must almost certainly have been introduced by someone, somehow – who does these things, and why?) have become visible, and a trapping programme has been initiated by Scottish Natural Heritage.

The RSPB tends not to talk about the impact of growing populations of raptors and other predatory birds, such as skuas, on other bird species. In this case, I am inclined to believe that there has been no significant increase in predatory birds over the recent and relevant period. I suppose, however, that it may be possible, with the very evident decline in the number of seabirds, that aggressive species may have increased their predation on curlew eggs and chicks. Hoodie crows and ravens might also be an issue. The logic is clear and inescapable: if one food source declines, these successful and adaptable birds look elsewhere.

As I hope I have shown, the debate is complex. When we look at the Orkney landscape itself, some suggested factors for the decline in bird numbers may be dismissed with some confidence, while others may be relevant. Rather too often, wholesale land reclamation is cited as a cause of the reduction in numbers of some species or other, but as I have made clear earlier, large-scale conversion of moorland or wetland here declined significantly after the 1980s and is unlikely to be relevant.

Increased drainage is also cited, and in this context the increasing appearance, mentioned earlier, of ponds in the Orkney pasture must be pertinent. These new ponds may be the result of a number of factors. I have referred already to increased rainfall, and the reduction in the number of "drying" months. These would raise the water-table, allowing such ponds to appear. While wetland is generally considered to be a good habitat for waders (some of these ponds might eventually become small wetlands), the ponds may also reflect a growing compaction of the soil, which means it drains less well. This may imply that under the changing climatic conditions, some pasture can no longer cope with the density of stock established in the drier past. Such compacted, damper areas harbour fewer invertebrates, which makes them less attractive as feeding grounds for birds including curlew, lapwing, redshank and oystercatcher. Ultimately, this will reduce their numbers.

The increased drainage that the RSPB claims to have noticed may be seen, therefore, in this changing context, and there is some clear logic here too. The farmers see that their fields are wetter than they were, and so they renew their drains. Initially, this means that big open drains between fields will be redug, becoming deeper as they are cleared of the vegetation that accumulates over the years. This in itself lowers the water-table in surrounding areas, which may include some of the nice wetland corners; they become drier and are easier to reclaim. But, at the same time, where drains are not renewed, other small patches of wetland will increase in area, and this too has been seen over the past decades. This is a shifting scene, and one where precise statistics are not easily available. What can be unequivocally stated is that our landscape, carefully observed, still has a multitude of small patches of wetland, in addition to the much larger ones, including the Loons, the Loch o' Banks and Durkadale, (all within the Parish of Birsay), to name a few.

Such wetlands are difficult to walk in and, in any case, I would never enter them in spring or summer to avoid disturbing breeding birds. Large or small, they are part of the botanical richness of our land. I have already mentioned the orchids, irises, meadowsweet and marsh cinquefoil. Rafts of bogbean lend them an almost tropical luxuriance, and water mint makes them strongly aromatic. Much of this, along with the teeming birdlife, may be seen from the few hides – we need rather more!

We are short of land mammals. One important creature, the Orkney vole, is happiest in areas of rough pasture, a habitat that does not appear to be under much threat here. Uncut rough grassland may be encountered outside fences, between fields, on cliff edges and around some ancient monuments such as the Ring of Brodgar. In these places, vole holes and runs are often seen. The Orkney vole is much larger than the field vole found in much of Britain, and is an important element in the diet of the hen harrier and short-eared owl, birds for which Orkney is noted. Although voles seem to tolerate quite wet ground, it is probable that cold, wet springs make life harder for them, as well as for the birds that prey on them. A decline in harrier numbers has been linked to a possible reduction in the number of voles, and the trend in the weather may well be implicated in both. Again, however, I feel that skua activity may be a factor. Both skuas and harriers share the same breeding grounds, and harrier nests, located in the heather, are open to the sky. Is it a coincidence that the numbers of harriers have declined as those of skuas have increased? And, as I have indicated before, a shortage of seabirds must have forced the skuas to look elsewhere. They are often now the dominant birds on the moors, and it is hard to overstate their belligerent nature. In the end, however, it was probably the big heath fire in Hoy that caused our pair of golden eagles to leave the islands, probably for good. I had often watched them trying to lead a normal life, under the very real handicap of being constantly harried by up to eight great skuas. And while I hope that the young pair of sea eagles that recently attempted to breed in the same island may be successful, it will certainly be interesting to see whether they get the same treatment!

Hoy might well be described as "mostly moorland", while Rousay has extensive areas of hill, and Westray and Eday have quite a lot of heather. From the Ring of Brodgar, the basin of the West Mainland is bounded by higher ground: from Yesnaby down to Stromness, in the hills of Orphir and round almost to Finstown, and from there in a great arc that nearly reaches the coast by the Loch of Swannay. The easiest way to experience this very different and remarkably unpopulated landscape is to take the road from Dounby over to Evie. This is another Orkney.

Four

In the Hill

Our little business, the Orkney Field and Arts Centre, was based in the small settlement beside the extensive ruins of the Earls' Palace in Birsay, where a medium-sized burn ran through the cutwaters of an old bridge into the wide, westward-facing bay. No one ever thought to refer to it as a river, but perhaps we should have, as it is Orkney's major water-course. (Rivers were one thing that I definitely did miss in the years I lived here). It can be traced quite far inland; the first section runs up from the village, past the fine mill of Boardhouse, to the medium-sized loch of that name, which occupies a broad valley between the ridge of Ravie Hill to the south, and the eminence of Kirbister Hill to the north. This is a rich, fertile and green area, even by Orkney standards, and it seems to have long been regarded as a desirable place to live. The "Boardhouse" name is part of this. It indicates the "house" (meaning the farm) that supplied the "bord" or table of the local magnate, in this case, the Earl himself when residing locally – much more of this anon.

At the eastern end of the loch is a low-lying area, some of which is rather rougher ground, but it has again been long inhabited and worked. If we continue to make our way upstream towards the smaller Loch of Hundland, we pass the farm of Kirbister. The buildings here are attractive and old, the house having a central hearth, but the name itself, "the church farm", may take us back to the early years of the second millennium AD, when the first country churches were frequently established beside major farms. There is now no sign of the church, but the farm has a wonderful feeling of antiquity and is maintained by the Orkney Museums Service.

Close to where the burn leaves the loch of Hundland, to flow into Boardhouse, is the entry point of another burn, which drains the long hills to the east. This is Durkadale, the dark valley, which must indeed have been very dark before large areas of heather were reclaimed and it became green. This area is simply called Hillside, and the stream is the Burn of Hillside. It flows gently through an important wetland, which is well worth observing from the single-track road. I always park at a convenient gate, where a track runs up to a low cottage. I used to do this rather blithely, as a remote cousin (and friend) of mine lived here, and was not exactly worried if I blocked her access for a few minutes, but I now have to remember that, sadly, she is no longer with us, and the house belongs to others.

The valley opens out as you drive eastwards and meet the road that cuts across the hills from Evie, heading down towards Dounby. Close to the junction, a smaller burn runs from the north, to join the first, and there is a parking space at the roadside. Here I would often leave our minibus, and take a group across the first field following the signs for the "Click Mill". This is a most attractive small building, of a type probably introduced by the Vikings when their first farmers settled in the islands, some time after 800 AD. It is simple, but clever in design. A single vertical shaft is turned by a small, horizontal paddle-type wheel set in a narrow culvert. The shaft rises up through the central hole of the lower mill-stone – again, of course, horizontal – and turns the upper stone, which rests on the one below. This is all housed within a neat little sandstone building, roofed with slabs and turf, somehow a rather self-possessed little structure, slightly recessed into the burn bed within the huge wide sweep of the surrounding bare hills. After I had explained how the mill worked and its historical significance, we would normally pause awhile in order to allow everyone to take photographs, or to look out for the famed hen harriers of the Orkney moorland. We nearly always saw our first of the day around here, rocking slightly as it flew low over the heather, the conspicuous white ring of the tail a great aid to locating a brown bird (if female) within a predominantly brown landscape. The male is much more easily spotted – light grey, almost a blue.

Then we would cross a little clapper bridge, and follow the side burn down to the main one, which this far up has changed its name (if not its nature) to the Burn of Rusht. It is not very wide at this point, and fairly shallow, and I was always hoping to see a dipper somewhere along here, but sadly never did. Then, for a while, we simply followed the burn deeper into the hills. It is always very quiet here; one aspect of Orkney that I appreciated enormously after living in the Highlands was that there were never any low-flying jet aircraft here to shatter the peace. But other things sometimes did...

By this time it would normally be around eleven in the morning, and as I knew that the real walking had not yet begun and I wanted to give my group a rest before it did, I would declare that it was coffee time, generally a most welcome pronouncement. On one occasion, the next few moments were both nerve-racking and hectic, the calm being shattered by piercing screams from one of our number. She had, in one movement, chucked her anorak on the ground in order to sit on it, and tried to do exactly that. The short-eared owl on which she was trying to sit, was, however, quite vehement in its disapproval of her intention and flew straight up at her behind. Order was eventually restored after we had ascertained that neither had suffered, as far as we could easily tell, any injury. Short-eared owls fly by day, and are the other "target species" in these moorland places. They have beautiful plumage and wonderful, cat-like faces with huge eyes, which give rise to their local name of "cattie-face".

The sheer profusion of common wildflowers can be so special here; thyme, tormentil, buttercups, milkwort, self-heal, heath bedstraw, lousewort, ladies' mantle and orchids, like a little alpine meadow beside the flowing water. Up on the hill we saw the insectivorous sundew and butterwort, while the intense colour of the bell heather was beginning to show along the drier banks.

We carried on along this burn till we reached a wider hollow. There seemed to be no significant remains of any building, such as another mill, here, but there was a stone stairway up the northern, steep side of the little amphitheatre. It was small, and narrow, and for no good reason, I thought of it always as the "Pictish stair". It was, however, more probable that the little hollow had been used for keeping stock in the days when the moors were exploited, and that the steps were to enable the herdboys or girls to climb up and down the steep slope. Be that as it may, we carefully climbed up them, and onto the sweep of hill above. From here we began to walk higher than the next – and ultimate – tributary burn, as it flowed from a bog, the breeding ground of a considerable number of greater black-backed and other gulls. This is a distinctly noisy and sometimes intimidating place. During all this time we would have been on the lookout for another bird, one with a well-deserved reputation for being even more aggressive – the dark, blunt, ominous-looking great skua or "bonxie". They frequently flew over these hills, as a shortcut between the Sound of Eynhallow and the western sea, but were also beginning to establish similar breeding colonies, which they would defend fiercely. As their numbers increased for many years after this, I was, on subsequent visits, sometimes made very abruptly aware that they had taken over somewhere new. They are large, powerful birds, and make a direct attack. I always walked these moors with a stick, and was, on occasion, very glad of its protection. I never actually hit one of the skuas, but they certainly hit me!

There were also many Arctic skuas nesting in the hills, some of them the extremely handsome white-fronted birds (which are known as "pale phase"), and we would hear, and occasionally see, golden plover and even, once or twice, a grouse.

This area, on a good day (and I went there only when it appeared to be set fair), was wonderfully open and spacious, a huge expanse of thin heather and moorland grasses, the only sign of the hand of man being the dark lines of old peat banks. At that point, I had spent much of my life walking on precisely this sort of soft, bouncy ground, and I revelled in it. Others, from other environments, found it much harder going, and I had to learn to moderate my natural pace. Fortunately, it was never a hardship to stop and wait for others to catch up; there was always something to look at, or for, among the wide horizons, bounded in one direction by the blue hills of Hoy.

In this trackless walk over the hill, I was heading for an objective that I knew existed, but was unseen. I intended, too, that it should remain unseen until the last possible moment, as it was a small lochan where I very much hoped there would be birds, which I really did not want to disturb. I had, therefore, established a route that approached the lochan from below, the last few yards of which went through old peat-cuttings. At this point I always insisted that the group should lie down and wriggle their way forward until they could see the peaty waters ahead of them. Luckily, this never failed to produce wonderful views of those extremely beautiful birds of the far North, the red-throated divers. Here, we always saw some close up, and on one memorable occasion, no fewer than fourteen, an unforgettable experience. While enjoying these splendid sights, my group were normally able to forget the last few moments of discomfort when they had been crawling over very soggy peat. That most amazing occasion, with so many of these wonderful birds, took their breath away, and they simply concentrated on the beauty in front of them, while I mused quietly on the perversity of life in general. I had been insisting that we should crawl on our final approach to the lochan, in order not to disturb the divers on the water – and we did not disturb them. Neither, apparently, did the boy in the canoe, floating among them, nor the tractor, with its peat-laden trailer, which was making its slow way along a track on the far bank.

(If in doubt, one should, of course, always err on the side of caution, minimising disturbance – but occasionally, it turns out to be superfluous!)

From here, we headed west, rounding a gentle eminence, then took the long descent back towards the mill and the parked minibus. It is possible that some of the group might have preferred me to cross to the line of the road, and follow it, but no one ever said anything, and as the line I was taking was actually significantly shorter, we never took to the tarmac. The hill beyond that road, on its western side, is simply called "Mid Hill", but it was very significant to me. It was there, like many others at this time, that I could cut peat, and did so every year of our time in the islands.

I had first learned how to cut and stack peat as a boy in Assynt, when we had gone to help Dannie the shepherd from the neighbouring house in Glenleraig. Both my brother and I were quite neat with our hands, and our first attempt at stacking met with his genuine approval, followed by a handwritten Certificate of Competence, which I kept until it had totally faded. Again, when living later in Assynt, I had cut our own peats, and had to carry each laborious sackful on my back an awkward distance to the road. It was therefore quite a relief to discover that the peat bank that went with our house here was, like many others on the hill, reached by a perfectly decent, dry track, and I could park my car exactly beside the scene of activity.

Although the aroma of it when burning is lovely, and there is something very attractive about winter warmth that costs only the physical effort to win it, there is nothing in the least romantic about the cutting of peat. Having removed the layer of vegetation and roots from the surface, and placed them, however roughly, on the area cut last year, you find yourself poised on a slippery, slimy, sort-of-level, into which you are supposed to cut – below your own feet. You have to do this, of course, without over-balancing. I have a long back, and most of the traditional tools for the purpose seem designed for smaller folk, so I would have to bend too far down, rapidly acquiring a sore back in the process. Having cut into this year's newly exposed bank, you then leap lightly down to the lower level, and chuck all the new-cut blocks onto the heather above where you have been working. At this point, you discover that new-cut peat is more liquid than solid, that it slides through your hands constantly, that you are forever losing it and having to bend down for it again. Having moved all the fresh-cut stuff, you then leap lightly up onto the bank to do it all again – and again, and again. At the end of the day, you are very tired, and feel that you will never, for the rest of your life, be able to stand up straight.

By the time I had arrived in Orkney, I was something of an "apprentice" naturist, but I soon accepted that neither the topography nor the climate of my new home was particularly encouraging for this. It was only up here on the deserted peat hill that I was able regularly, if briefly, to strip. There were a few Aprils with a spell of genuinely warm weather when I was able to do so. It gave me a wonderful feeling of contentment, and I would sit on the dry edge of a heather bank, drinking a cup of thermos coffee, resting from my exertions with the warm air around my naked body, listening to the distant curlew music and looking to the enamel-clear blues and greens of the distant farmland. I could hear meadow pipits and skylarks, and watch the harriers hunt low along the heather strips where the voles might be lurking. This was the island spring and it made my heart glad.

Five

The Long Story Begins

One of the most obvious (but still perhaps the most astonishing) things about Orkney is its architectural history. For a small group of northern islands, nowadays often perceived as remote, and with only a moderate population, it has an unsurpassed heritage. It seems there are fascinating and attractive monuments to study from almost every period. Note that I use the word "architectural" for very valid reasons. In so many other places, although archaeological sites exist, many are simple post-holes, or stains in the soil, perhaps a scatter of tools. We have those too, but we also have substantial buildings, which tell us much about the lives of the previous inhabitants of the archipelago, our ancestors. We can see where they slept, where they sat, where they cooked, and where they buried their dead. Perhaps most astonishing of all, there is detailed evidence of their sophistication, their interest in colour and design, their conceptual and organisational abilities. Orkney tells us much about human endeavour through time.

Most likely, it is when I try to describe its archaeology that my attempts to write about Orkney may be seen as something approaching cheek. I understand this perfectly; there are many far better qualified than I to write upon this ever-expanding subject. To keep abreast of all the discoveries still being made, sites being surveyed or excavated, and theories being advanced, would amount to a full-time job in itself. I therefore make it plain that I have probably only two qualifications for venturing to do so. One is nothing less than devotion. I have thought and dreamed of Orkney's archaeology, photographed and talked about it since I was a schoolboy. The other is that throughout all the years I have been introducing groups of people from all walks of life to these wonderful monuments, I have had to observe, to think, to order my thoughts, to present them cogently to professionals as well as amateurs – perhaps most important of all, I have had to answer their questions. There are some things I have come to believe, and some things I have noticed, as well as others about which I still wonder. This is all I offer, but it is done with sincerity, and some humility – most of the time!

The slowly rising seas will have obliterated, at least from easy view, the places where the first settlers landed, and where, for much of the time they probably lived. The prosperous activity of succeeding periods, whether Neolithic or Victorian, will also have done much to hide the activity of those early hunter-gatherers. But we can at least deduce that the islands offered them many resources; they must have flourished. Seals on the shore, fish in the sea and lochs, deer presumably over most of the land, and above all, birds. Birds on the shores, the cliffs, the lochs, including the thousands of geese and duck that gather in the autumn and winter. The climate was improving, too, and there may have been enough woodland to provide alder or willow poles for constructing light shelters; I am still inclined to wonder about the adequacy of winter dwellings in what must always have been a windy climate.

The same rising waters must also conceal any remains of the boats that brought the first farmers, and, perhaps with rather more difficulty, their stock. I worry about these boats, or at least about the idea of setting forth across the fierce currents of the Pentland Firth, whether on a raft or in some kind of coracle, sharing what can, surely, have been only a rather confined space, with cows, or at least calves, sheep and perhaps a few other creatures. But somehow they did it. The first farmers actually arrived here, at the islands they could see from the North Coast.

When they did so is not particularly clear. In the most general terms, the New Stone Age or Neolithic in the islands is said to have begun around 4000 BC. But it has to be remarked that we have accomplished stone buildings – such as the houses at Knap of Howar in Papa Westray or the great tombs of Rousay – that date from only a few hundred years later, and these certainly do not look like anyone's first attempt to build in stone. Are there shaky, earlier prototype houses or tombs lurking somewhere? Or did these folk settle in the archipelago (spreading out over its significant extent), organise their agriculture and prosper quickly in the established climatic optimum, rapidly acquiring skills in building with stone? I do not know, but I am sure that they must have observed how well the folk they found there were living, and copied their habits of hunting and fishing, scaling the tall cliffs for eggs and seafowl, gathering shellfish and even seaweed on the coast. With the stock and crops they had brought to the islands, all this made for a varied and nutritious diet and, in addition, they clearly had time to build stone structures with care and skill. In some ways, at least, this looks like a good life.

What are, at the moment anyway, our oldest buildings, those at Knap of Howar, in every way begin perfectly our long story of human habitation on Orkney. For a start, this farmstead is astonishingly well-preserved, its walls standing to a height of nearly five feet. It clearly reveals the comparative comfort and spaciousness of domestic life at this time, being a dwelling-house with an interconnecting and adjoining building, which probably served a number of purposes, including that of a barn. There are stone benches, partitions made of vertical flagstones, and I hope that you can still see the stone quern for grinding the cereals that these farming folk grew. All this allows even the most prosaic of individuals to start to imagine aspects of their lives. But I think there is more here than just the physical structure; there is an almost spiritual quality that derives not only from the buildings' very survival, but also from the stone itself. Like so many Orcadian buildings, the stone is a comforting ochre colour, and the contrast between the vertical slabs that divide the space and the neat, horizontally laid stonework of the walls increases that spiritual feeling. This may be seen by some as rather fanciful, but it is felt, I think, in many of Orkney's buildings.

Knap of Howar used to be quoted as having been built around 3850 BC, but in some texts at least it has since "slipped" slightly, and is now listed as 3600 BC, a difference that worries me very little. I shall always be very approximate in any dates I use, partly to avoid giving a spurious sense of precision in a discipline where all dating is subject to a margin of error. What really matters, I feel, is that these structures are truly very old, probably the oldest stone buildings in Europe.

Perhaps only a couple of centuries later, we can see the continuation of that method of construction with vertical slabs and horizontally laid walls on a bigger scale, in the tombs of Rousay, culminating in the great monument of Midhowe. This is one of the most impressive structures of the archipelago, though the fragility of much of its stonework has necessitated a hangar-like cover. Luckily, that does little to detract from its atmosphere and impact, unlike the concrete protecting other tombs on the island. None of the roofs from this type of tomb survive, but the supporting slabs of Midhowe increase in height towards the centre, presumably in an attempt to shed water.

What can clearly be seen at Midhowe is that, large though the initial building was, at some stage it was made even bigger with the addition of more material, the outer stones of which were laid in a decorative herring-bone type of pattern. This is particularly clear beside the entrance. This habit of making significant monuments in the landscape even larger is seen elsewhere, notably at Camster in nearby Caithness, and hints at the aspirations and organisation of the population at the time. What is not at all obvious is why one location on Rousay, a hilly island that can never have been well-populated in comparison with others, should have been chosen for this great effort of construction.

It is salutary to recall that Walter Grant, the whisky-making archaeologist laird of the island, told my grandmother that when he had announced that he intended to dig at Midhowe, he had been, however gently, mocked. Everyone believed that the grassy, unploughed ridge was natural. Down-washed soil, caused by natural drainage and years of ploughing on the slopes above had effectively disguised the location of the great tomb (some are still being found simply because a farmer has decided to plough his sloping field in a different direction). I have the excavation report that he signed when he presented it to my grandmother. It makes clear that a dry-stone dyke (probably Victorian and associated with the large new farm of that era) ran along its crest, obscuring the real shape of the mound. Although a short line of stones was visible elsewhere, they were assumed to be part of an earlier such field wall.

Perhaps 500 years later, the best-known and most-loved domestic site in Orkney was being built. Skara Brae, like Knap of Howar, is amazingly well-preserved, and set in the beautiful wide sweep of the Bay of Skaill. Here again the charm resides in the old stones, the sophisticated construction of the walls, and the visible detail of what we might nowadays call the fixtures and fittings: the mural cells, the cubby-holes in the walls, beds and hearths, little tanks and grinding basins, and, above all perhaps, the elegant dressers or sideboards. You can imagine everyday life carrying on, presumably with little privacy, but both domestic and practical.

This village was built in two phases. The larger houses that dominate the site were constructed over the foundations of earlier, significantly smaller dwellings. What actually happened between the two phases of construction is one of the most surprising elements of the site, and it is a shame that it is now significantly harder to see than it used to be. After reducing the earlier houses to a few courses of stone, the villagers planned and constructed a system of stone-walled drains that run under the walls and floors of the later structures, heading in the direction of what is now the bay. Whether the purpose of these well-constructed drains was simply to lower the water-table and keep the floors dry, or rather more elaborate than that, is hard to decide, but in some houses a flagstone in the floor may be lifted, giving access to the drain. Whether this was to function as a kitchen sink, or even a loo, is probably a matter of conjecture, and perhaps depends on the flow of water available. But the possibilities remain, and are proof of the sophistication of the villagers. (I was once explaining this to a group, one member of whom said, rather grumpily perhaps, that Manchester got public drainage in 1864 AD – (I have never checked the date!) – which enabled me to quip that civilisation was a slow process that spread from north to south.)

This important feature used to be visible via two hatches in the turf. One is now firmly locked, and the other replaced by a grille that makes it almost impossible to see any detail, which is rather a shame. Another feature now barred from view is the striking interior of what used to be called Hut Number Seven (I prefer to refer to these sophisticated homes as houses). It has furnishings similar to those of the others, but the dresser is particularly elegant, and the edge of at least one of the beds has clear marks in the stone, which might be designs or carvings of some kind. Under that bed the skeletons of two old women were found. We may find this somewhat gruesome, but perhaps the idea was that the spirits of the ancestors were there with the occupants – who knows? This house was covered with a glass roof, through which the interior could be viewed, but this has since been replaced and is now turf-covered, denying any sight of this iconic space. Photographs of the house feature in many accounts of Skara Brae, but there are very few at the site itself. The justification for this change was that apparently the stonework was suffering as a result of the heat of the sun through the glass roof. I hanker after a slightly more imaginative solution than simply closing off the structure: is it not possible nowadays to regulate easily the temperature and humidity? And in the interim, the little modern building close by could perhaps house some good, big illustrations of what we are currently missing.

Skara Brae is now both famous and very accessible, which can make the site and visitor centre extremely busy, and may reduce the quality of the whole experience. The number of visiting (and very large) liners that appear every summer certainly exacerbates this problem, although this increase in ships bringing visitors to Orkney and the famous sites seems to be very much welcomed in some quarters. It is clear that the growth in visitor numbers cannot simply be maintained for ever. It must ultimately result in some damage to the structures on site, although I know that these are carefully monitored. Surely Historic Environment Scotland does not need to be reminded that success cannot be measured simply by the numbers that pass through any site, but also in the admittedly more difficult measure of the quality of the visitor's experience at any one location? Perhaps when the next domestic Neolithic site is excavated, thought (and funding) might be given early on to its subsequent presentation to the public? (We will return to this topic.) In this connection I have wondered whether the time is not now right to consider a re-excavation (and wider exploration) of the contemporary village of Rinyo on Rousay. This would be with a view to opening the monument to public visitation and reinforcing the archaeological importance of this relatively accessible island, as well as adding to our understanding of this significant site. As far as I can tell from contemporary photographs, the actual structures are not as well-preserved as those at Skara Brae, but many of the same features are present, including the drains, with the interesting additions of clay ovens.

At another famous site of this period, the question of restricting access had to be addressed some time ago, and visitors now enjoy Maeshowe in limited parties. This remarkable structure is not only enormously impressive, but suggests much about the capabilities of the people who planned and organised its construction. Apart from its scale, and that of the stones employed in the building, the quality of the masonry is superb, and, so far, unequalled in the archipelago or further afield. Here, the true potential of the Orkney sandstone is realised.

Appreciating the aesthetic quality of this building is one thing, understanding quite how it was built is another. The debate continues about the source of the stones, and how they were brought from the quarries to the site. These arguments also apply to the stone circles, of which also more anon. While most of us are familiar with the idea of erecting the individual stones used in the circles (and it has been done experimentally, with ramps, pits, ropes and a fair amount of labour), it seems clear to me that the construction of Maeshowe was significantly more difficult, and the methods utilised far more elusive. It is possible to imagine that, in the construction of a reasonably simple, dolmen-type structure, it is feasible to jack up the corners of the large, flattish stone that will become the roof, and then to place some supporting stones under it, before letting the roof down until it rests on them. I have wondered whether this principle might have been employed in the construction of the extraordinary entrance passage, the sides and roof of which are each one enormous long slab. It would require real precision in placing the side slabs and some way of assessing the levels, and I have to say that it seems to me unlikely. When it comes, however, to the construction of the corbelled roof, I do not believe that this simple idea of slowly levering up the great stones is an adequate explanation of the very neat way they sit, one course projecting a short distance above the one below. To me, it looks as if each block of sandstone were actually lowered on to the one below. I am certain that they cannot have simply been pushed from the back (of each side) until they were considered in a suitable position. Apart from the possibility of friction and weight making that extremely difficult, the pinning-stones (or "pinners") would make it impossible. If we are correct in saying that these minutely thin, long stones that lie between the huge slabs and are flush with the external surfaces were so placed to ensure a perfect level for the next slab to rest on, they would simply have been pushed out of the way by the movement of that upper slab. They would then have to be pushed back, and hammered flat, and, on careful inspection, it does not look to me as if that had been done.

But I am no expert, and the question of its construction is hardly solved in the above discussion. If the big slabs were indeed lowered, how was this achieved? I really have no answer. What the mystery does at least emphasise is that Maeshowe was an immense achievement. There is debate as to whether these chambered tombs were originally constructed with this purpose in mind, although we know, of course, that some time after their initial construction, many were so used. The question is raised in an entertaining and thought-provoking new book about the archaeology of a neighbouring county – *Caithness Archaeology: Aspects of Prehistory* by Andrew Heald and John Barber – but Maeshowe is of little help in such a discussion. It was virtually empty when excavated, and could easily have combined two possible functions. Bodies could have been placed in the side-chambers, as indeed seems very likely, but the impressive central space, lit as is so well-known by the light of the setting sun at the midwinter solstice, would have been perfectly suitable for any kind of associated ritual, and was, perhaps, a temple in itself.

That impressive space has for long years been diminished in stature, as far as I am concerned, by the fact that much of the roof, which is neither original nor constructed in the same fashion as the supporting walls and corbelling, has been painted a glaring white. It is ugly and distracting, and quite unnecessary. No one would be in danger of thinking that it was part of the ancient structure if they could not see it. I proposed many years ago to the then head of Historic Scotland that it should be repainted in the darkest possible matt brown, with downlights angled to focus on specific features, in the way that the current custodians do with a torch. I was told that this idea did not chime with Historic Scotland's plans for the site, although with the new institutional structure, perhaps times have changed?

Times were changing then. Maeshowe embodies the first consistent use of the immense stones we call megaliths, but it was followed shortly after by the extraordinary creation of the two stone circles, the Stones of Stenness and the Ring of Brodgar, along with many other features, some now less obvious than they were. This whole area between the two major lochs of Orkney, that of Harray and Stenness, seems to have been laid out almost as a designed (or sacred?) landscape, of which the circles were obviously a principal focus of effort, and presumably, of subsequent, "special" activity. Stenness came first, but what you actually see there is now as much about presentation as about content, and I will simply comment here that its erection seems to have been so "satisfactory", for whatever reasons, that it was decided to erect another, significantly larger, not far away. In itself, given the effort involved, this was an extraordinary decision.

Brodgar is an imposing feature in the landscape, and appears as the focus of the isthmus between the lochs. People tend to react quite strongly to it, and in many different ways. My mother, who was stationed in Orkney during the Second World War, said that when a number of girls and men were driving past at night, on their way to a dance at one of the camps, most of the girls got out and wandered around the dark stones in the moonlight. All of the men, hardened servicemen, one would have thought, stayed firmly in the safety of the truck. I have frequently sat with a group on one of the adjoining mounds, and watched others make their way around the circle. On one occasion, we saw a man walk briskly up to one stone, hug it enthusiastically, and then carry on, with apparently undiminished enthusiasm, to hug all the rest. Billy Connolly, you may recall, stripped here and ran naked around the stones. On another occasion, we had to walk carefully to avoid a large number of folk, vaguely spread-eagled across and around the perimeter path. They were presumably plugging themselves into the local energy circuit, or some such thing.

These strange activities have about as much validity as any other. The truth is we have very little idea why this huge effort of excavation (of the surrounding ditch) and erection (of the perhaps sixty stones) was ever even contemplated, let alone begun and completed. I once had a long discussion on this topic with that much-missed and most agreeable of Scottish archaeologists, Graham Ritchie, who was staying in our house in Birsay along with his wife Anna (of whom more to come) and their enchanting children. The astronomical theories of Professor Thom were at the time much debated, but it turned out that Graham, who had excavated Stenness, was not convinced by them. We must, of course, accept that there is some relatively simple astronomical significance to specific monuments of this period, such as Maeshowe and Stonehenge, but it is very hard to see what celestial imperative would encourage one to progress from the project to erect the postulated twelve stones of Stenness to the possible sixty of Brodgar. We both felt that the purpose could have been as much social as astronomical. Graham said that they might have danced around the stones, or held agricultural shows within them. The reference to agriculture is itself very apt. One of the ideas proposed by Professor Thom and his supporters was that the circles could have been lunar calendars, and it was often claimed that such a calendar would have been a necessity for the everyday purposes of fishermen and farmers. Quite how the unfortunate beings who did not have access to such monuments were supposed to cope, I have no idea, but the notion is itself an academic's fancy, not a common-sense thought. Fishermen who live by the sea observe it from day to day, and know when the tides are increasing or otherwise, while farmers are well aware that the calendar has nothing to do with the suitability of the day, or the soil, for some planned activity such as sowing. After the dreadful summer of 2015, few Orcadian farmers put their animals out because a specific date in the calendar had been reached – the fields were in no fit state, and that was the deciding factor.

Two aspects of Brodgar never seem to be discussed in print (or if they ever have been, it has escaped my notice). One is very clear. The circle is laid out on a bit of ground that is obviously slanting towards the Loch of Harray. Why should this be so? There is plenty of space on the isthmus for a level site, and the decision must surely have been deliberate. I have yet to make any sense of it. The other is much more subtle, but I can hardly credit that I should be the only person ever to experience it. When Graham Ritchie excavated Stenness, he laid bare the hearth in the centre of the circle, but there always seems to be agreement that there is nothing at the centre of Brodgar. Accordingly, I have very rarely walked there (partly in an effort to reduce any human impact on the moorland vegetation inside the circle), but

I once had a group that included a man who was very deeply into the astronomical theories. He was, however, very practical in out-look, and wanted to see whether there might be any clear alignments from the centre of the ring, perhaps with obvious features on the skyline. We therefore walked towards the centre, with me leading, and, somewhat inevitably, talking as I went, perhaps pointing out the varieties of heather to be found there. As I reached a certain point, it happened. My voice was noticeably amplified, the sound bouncing off the stones, which, suddenly, were functioning as acoustic panels. Had this ability been discovered after Stenness was finished, and was this property so valued that it was decided to proceed with a much bigger monument, which would permit greater (much greater) gath-erings to listen... to someone? Again, I have little idea, and it would in any case be hard to prove, but the experience was valid and gen-uine, another aspect of this fascinating place. The weather conditions were not out of the ordinary, it was certainly not blowing a gale, but neither was it possessed of some unearthly calm.

In those days, I often wondered about the little hill further down the isthmus towards the causeway between the lochs, by the cottage with two standing stones in its immediate garden, but I never saw anything in the field before that cottage to make me think it might be hiding something. It is in that field that the astonishing and complex site known as the Ness of Brodgar is currently being excavated, and as every year brings to light more fascinating aspects, its importance grows. As I have no connection with the excavation, and a real effort is being made by the team involved to make their progress widely available, I will attempt no description, and confine myself to three thoughts.

The first is that the buildings being uncovered are now often described as "temples". However, in that context, I have never seen any current reference to a structure in Shetland, roughly similar in plan if not in construction, that was referred to in the book on the Northern Isles that so inspired my youth. This was firmly classed then as a temple, and I have visited it. It is at Stanydale, and another at Yoxie was associated with it. Both were then compared with Neolithic temples in Malta. Revised dating and new thinking may make a nonsense of all this, but I would love to know!

The whole area under discussion, which feels like the very heart of the West Mainland, the largest land mass in the islands, is turning out to be of enormous significance, and early enough in date to have influenced social and cultural developments much further south. Much conventional archaeological thinking is thus being turned on its head. It was assumed that ideas, perhaps people also, had moved from south to north, but now the possibility of a flow of ideas in the other direction is being discussed. Perhaps my quip about civilisation moving south was not wide of the mark!

Finally, the extent and importance of these discoveries make me extremely anxious. I hope that attention is being paid to the critical imperative of ultimately displaying the site at the Ness of Brodgar to the public? For the casual visitor, nothing has the emotional impact of "old stones". Skara Brae touches the heart, in a way that the stone-and-turf plan of the contemporary village of Barnhouse does not. Ness of Brodgar is a hugely important site; we do not have the right to destroy it, and deny its impact to others. I realise that there are extraordinary difficulties ahead, in terms of decision-making, in the further exploration of the site, in planning, in simply finding the space to make public access feasible, and, crucially, in reducing the impact on this beautiful location. There are, critically, the rights of the people most closely affected by the site and future proposals, which must be respected (two of them I am proud to call friends). BUT we must not lose this site.

Six

High Ground

In recent years, archaeologists have found indications that our ancestors had, at various times and in various locations, a true sense of
the end of an era. Sites, whether tombs in Orkney or caves in Skye,
have been closed up, filled with earth and all sorts of bits and pieces.
Sometimes, too, there has been evidence of feasting in the immediate neighbourhood. This is true of the complex of buildings at
Ness of Brodgar, and at least reinforces the view that these special
places acted as social centres, whatever other activities may have
been going on at other times. The idea, however, that people would
declare, somehow, that a turning-point had been reached, that things
would henceforth be different, and that this point in time should be
marked with great celebration, is puzzling to me. Who would decide
that this crucial point had been reached and why, and how did they
persuade so many others that these hitherto special, or sacred, places
should now be firmly put out of use?

From our current perspective, such turning-points are discerned
only in retrospect; the sole exceptions I can think of have been the
end of major wars, such as the First and Second World Wars, or the
oft-debated turn of the Millennium – an excuse for much special
celebration that now seems rather odd.

The strange thing about Ness of Brodgar's declared "end" is that
we can see, again with hindsight, that they were right: the good times
were coming to a close. The climate was changing, deteriorating,

becoming cooler, wetter and windier. It does seem that life must have become harder, crops more difficult to win, the soil increasingly waterlogged, sea-fishing more hazardous. There was no longer the capacity to feed a labour force engaged on big projects, and the grand designs ceased to be planned.

For us, the most obvious manifestation of the changing climate and times is the spread of peat across the increasingly waterlogged soil, the peat that remains on the hills of the islands. Living on higher ground may have become untenable, and it is likely that earlier structures are now at least partially buried. In Hoy, for instance, any agricultural land that might have supported a small community around the strange, rock-cut tomb known as the Dwarfie Stane has disappeared. But as you walk towards it after crossing the wide valley floor, there is at least one slab set upright (which could never happen naturally), and the hint of a few more. These sweeping moors of Hoy are now being explored, with a view to discovering exactly how much archaeologically significant material has so far escaped notice in the heather.

Hoy has a very special atmosphere. It is the Highlands of Orkney, and we have always enjoyed a day out in its wilds. When I was young, and the groups who came to us were rather fitter than they tend to be now, we often spent a day on the island without using a minibus at all. We would make an early start and take the little passenger ferry from Stromness (passing the small isle of Graemsay), to the pier at Mo Ness, from where we would walk. This north end has good agricultural land under the imposing Ward Hill, and there is comfrey growing freely on the verges of the narrow road. We would always head first for the Dwarfie Stane, past an attempt at a conifer plantation; this has since been felled and replaced with largely native trees. In this section, we would see many small birds: wrens, stonechats, chaffinches. One time, we thought we heard long-tailed tits. We were always looking out for harriers as we crossed to the tomb, and the occasional merlin appeared. Once up at the monument, having admired the stubborn perseverance that must have been required to hollow out its chamber from the great block of sandstone, we would hang around for a while – just in case. More than once, our patience was rewarded as a golden eagle appeared over the band of cliff that dominates the site, the Dwarfie Hamars. On one occasion, it appeared exactly on cue, overhead, before landing on a project-ing rock and posing in a ridiculously impressive style, with the sun highlighting the gold of its nape. When it eventually flew off, a raven obligingly mobbed it, providing us with both a sense of scale and real action. As I turned to say something, two of the group, middle-aged and serious you would say, were embracing, tears in their eyes. They had just had an experience they would never forget.

Then, if we were all feeling really fit, we headed for the steep slopes of Ward Hill. These effectively banish any sense that Orkney is flat, and we were generally speechless as we puffed our way uphill. But, like all ascents, it does come to an end, and we could walk its high ridge. From the summit, the views were truly wonderful – the high points overlooking the archipelago are really special places. From here, we could see many of the islands, except the farthest of the North Isles, but it was the view south that was most dramatic, with the hills of Caithness and Sutherland clear and sharp in outline. To the west, we could see, too, small islands that are part of Orkney, but virtually never seen from there and rarely visited: Sule Skerry and Stack Skerry.

Being up in these high places does enable you to realise that you are part of a wider world , not as isolated as the winter gales may make you feel. A few times, from the heights of Rousay (Knitchen Hill on a couple of occasions, and the highest point of the road above Saviskaill Bay on another), we could see far to the north. On all occasions it was near the end of June, brilliantly clear, but with a genuinely cold northerly breeze, and there was no room for doubt: we could see the ridge of land that is the southern end of the long Shetland Mainland. (I have never seen this recorded in print, but it does at least show why early farmers also reached this remoter island group – they did know it was there!)

Having celebrated at the summit cairn, I would lead the group along the ridge southwards, descending slightly so that we could look down into the fine corrie of Nowt Bield. Here on a number of occasions we looked down on a pair of eagles, gliding along the steep contours below us, an unusual and splendid sight. After this, having drunk in the views from the southern end of the high ridge, we would turn westwards and descend the lower shoulder above the Red Glen. A number of what would be referred to as "dales" in most of Orkney are called "glens" here; this, coupled with the nearby name "Kinnaird", which is Gaelic in origin, must indicate a significant Highland influence at some period.

Hoy is a big island, and on a normal day trip you cannot visit everything. Folk are drawn to the spectacular sea-stack, the famous Old Man, and a brisk walk in that direction does give you splendid views of it and its matrix cliffs – you may have the added thrill of watching climbers inching their way up its vertical sides. An easier alternative lets you wander around Rackwick, with its great bay. This is the only break in the island's majestic west-coast cliffs, its beach of boulders pink and blue and, most years, a stretch of beautiful sand. The atmosphere here is hard to describe, but is felt by most visitors; perhaps there is a tinge of melancholy engendered by the now largely uncultivated fields, and by the small groups of cottages and farm buildings, a few still ruined but many lately restored. You will not be surprised to know that many photographers come here. It was also a favourite haunt of local artists such as Sylvia Wishart and the poet George Mackay Brown. The composer Peter Maxwell Davies lived for a long time in a cottage perched halfway up the cliff, looking out over the surging sea. A few of us were passing once, on a fine day, when he came out and chatted to us. He even showed us the neat, cosy interior of the little house, including the vital piano that had been carried up the long, steep path from the end of the narrow road. To my mind (not backed up by great musical knowledge), I feel his music acquired a telling simplicity during his years in Orkney. I hear piano pieces such as *Farewell to Stromness* and *Yesnaby Ground* and think immediately of the wide and glorious prospect from his door.

Sometimes, having descended from Ward Hill and enjoyed the views over Rackwick, we would return via the northern glen to the other side of the island, taking the track that wanders along beside the burn. If I felt that my group was up to it, we would cross over to the narrow throat of Berriedale and its little wood, and enjoy the childish adventure of struggling through deep heather into the close-growing birch, rowan, aspen, wild rose, stone bramble and honeysuckle of this magical place. Nearby, a large and healthy juniper was also thriving, all very different from the vegetation we had been seeing earlier in the week in Mainland. Once, we accidentally found a harrier's nest, wide open and obvious in the heather, very much at the mercy of any passing great skuas – and there were many of those! We took only the quickest of looks at the two young birds in the nest, one significantly larger than the other, before moving on. Once, we heard a cuckoo at precisely this point.

We soon discovered where all the bonxies were heading. In the Sandy Loch at the head of the glen there were no fewer than thirty-five of these imposing birds bathing, splashing, calling and constantly flying in and out, an amazing sight. The Sandy Loch is well named, as the track passes here through a genuine, large dune of the pinkest sand, quite a surprising feature in what generally appears a dampish landscape. From here, it is all downhill to the pier at Mo Ness, and easy walking, but the views are in any case enticing.

I have had many wonderful days in Hoy, and after one of these walks, I was moved, on my return home, to write a quick note in my journal:

"All the magic of the North was fixed in Hoy today; the colours, sharp in the northerly wind, were deep and clear, the sea and sky blazing with blue and white, the dark brown of the high-heaved shoulders of the steep hills, the clarity of streams running over sand, and above all, the host of road – and trackside flowers. There was tormentil, lemon-yellow on dark green, golden heads of hawkweed, gold-red of the beautiful (and slender) St John's wort, the aptly named eyebright, fairy-dancing flax, cushions of pale purple wild thyme, swathes of deepest crimson bell heather, as well as stone bramble, bog asphodel, heath spotted orchid and others. Berriedale dripped drifts of palest honeysuckle and blush-pink roses ... the hard light on the sea on the boat trip home, the wheel of a porpoise fin in the sun."

But that last sentence was anticipating slightly, because part of the beauty of this day was fixed in that slow descent to catch the wee ferry. Depending on the state of the tide and the weather, this part of North Hoy may be possessed by a truly ethereal beauty. The sea is very shallow and set with sand-bars, so that, like Waulkmill Bay, the water may be of the subtlest opal, as translucent as enamel.

Down by this shore, set back from the road, is a fine old house, in whose garden are enormous, wide-spreading sycamores. They used to serve a splendid afternoon tea here, and we would relax in this beautiful garden, by the magnificent trees, recovering from our exertions. Such days are unforgettable.

Seven

Low Ground

After many years living halfway up his cliff, Peter Maxwell Davies left the High Island and went to live in Sanday, the lowest island in Orkney. Many years ago, I spent a few days there with the Scottish Society for Northern Studies, and what I most remember from that visit are the endless stretches of sand, the low-lying land behind, almost below the sea and subdued under the immense sky. A look at old maps seems to suggest that the island is hardly solid, that it shifts in shape as the winds blow, joining small areas of more substantial rocky island, with tenuous beaches and dunes – built up one winter, breached and destroyed another. There ought to be old legends about this elusive island, where a perfect summer day can give you a glimpse of Eden, with quiet, fertile fields, drifts of wildflowers, brilliant flocks of birds, all set in a shimmering sea.

From that first visit, I recall a walk along one of the long head-lands, Els Ness, basically a low island joined to the rest by one of the many ayres, or storm beaches. It holds Sanday's most obvious ancient monument, the splendid tomb of Quoyness. This reminded me of one of my favourites, Cuween Hill chambered tomb, on the old high road from Kirkwall to Finstown. But the headland is also remarkable for a number of lumps and bumps and twistings of stone, the sort of elusive archaeology that sometimes requires the "eye of faith" to see at all (thank you, John Barber!), and a certain amount of optimism to count or survey. Estimates of how many of these mounds there actually are have varied a lot over the years. The general agreement, however, is that this is one of the archipelago's most significant sites from the period that followed the great days of the tombs, the era we call the Bronze Age. The long climatic downturn I have already mentioned may well have meant that such low, sandy headlands, remaining cultivable, were truly significant places, and thus they became embellished, over time, with these mounds or barrows.

To get a better idea of such sites it is useful to visit the Knowes of Trotty in the West Mainland, where one of the hills of the basin's rim runs into bogland. Recent investigation has suggested that there were actually sixteen barrows here. Some of these are very obvious, and one seems to dominate the others. It retains a stone cist (basically a box made up of slabs), set at the top of an artificial mound. This is itself located, apparently, on a natural rise that has been sculpted to give the appearance of a kerb running around the base of the structure.

A local antiquarian excavated this very obvious mound in 1858, and the contents of the cist remain one of the most spectacular finds of Orcadian archaeology: four gold, roughly circular shapes now endowed with the name of "sun discs"; twenty-seven amber beads; and some burnt human bones. The gold discs are patterned with concentric circles separated by repeated linear marks, the sort of design found on carved stones from Skara Brae or Ness of Brodgar. The gold and amber, neither of which would have been found naturally in Orkney, indicate trade and cultural links with other parts of Britain, perhaps even with Scandinavia. This makes it very clear that this is a high-status site, a burial place perhaps for community leaders.

I have always felt that these finds might shed some light on an aspect of the (much later) runic inscriptions within Maeshowe. They are quite well known, but the implications of some of the messages they seem to convey are still puzzling. A few refer unequivocally to a great treasure removed from the tomb. The large mound of Maeshowe has always been conspicuous in the landscape, and I can see no reason why it should not have been adopted for some subsequent purpose, maybe in the way that the Ring of Brodgar became a focus for the placing of a number of later barrows that can still be seen there. Perhaps it was actually used, filled with yet more gold and amber, which the Vikings would certainly have recognised as treasure? Given the subsequent history of the site, it is very hard to argue that Maeshowe was definitely never used during the Bronze Age, while other equally conspicuous sites within the same area clearly were.

As far as domestic sites of the period are concerned, the combination of severe weather during 2015 and the insubstantial nature of much of the coastline of Sanday has resulted in the uncovering of some fourteen "circular spreads of stone". These were found in the intertidal zone off another headland, that of Tres Ness (the next along the coast, to the east of Els Ness). They are Bronze Age houses, in a very significant settlement, made even more remarkable by the presence of a "large number of ard-points, stone mattocks, stone bars, hammerstones and stone-flaked knives" (University of the Highlands and Islands – Archaeology Institute blog). Some structures could be seen appearing from under the large sand dunes nearby, and much more of this amazing new site might yet remain safely covered by the blown sand. Those in the intertidal zone are, of course, at very real risk from the same forces that uncovered them. I have previously mentioned blown sand in Hoy; Sandwick, the area surrounding Skaill Bay, is covered by significant deposits of sand, as are the Links on which I lived in Birsay. Westray has similar expanses, all of which point to a period or periods when a combination of tides and high winds radically changed the appearance of parts of the archipelago.

(Somewhat ironically, just as I was writing the above in January 2016, there was a great deal of excitement in the southern news media about the discovery of "Britain's Pompeii", the uncovering of perhaps five wooden roundhouses in Cambridgeshire. These were declared to be "the best-preserved Bronze-Age dwellings ever found in the country". None of the reports, however, actually clarified whether "the country" was simply England, or whether they meant Britain, which would, of course, include Orkney. If the latter, it would be interesting to debate whether fourteen or more stone houses in Orkney are more significant than five or more wooden houses in Cambridgeshire – although the wooden and textile finds from the later, waterlogged site are certainly fascinating.)

That these changes, albeit on a smaller scale, can happen quite rapidly and within living memory, may be seen in a much more recent context – that of the construction of the Churchill Barriers during the Second World War. I will have more to say about these later, suffice it to point out here that since the construction of the Barrier across the open channel between Burray and South Ronaldsay, a combination of wind and tide has caused the deposition of a large area of sand, in part now well vegetated, on its eastern side.

If you take that route south across the Barriers, on to South Ronaldsay and keep going, eventually you will see signs for the Tomb of the Eagles, a fine chambered cairn above the island's low cliffs. It has become well-known, partly because of its interesting recent history, being excavated by the farmer on whose land it was, and partly because of its unique, hands-on interpretation carried out by the family of the same man. But another site on this farm of Liddle is in fact much more unusual than the tomb. That is the structure and associated heap now known as Liddle Burnt Mound, which probably dates from the mid to late Bronze Age. I well remember a cool, sunny day when I went there on my own, and was lucky enough to find Ronnie Simison, the farmer and owner of the site, actually on duty there. We had a long talk about it, and several other aspects of Orcadian archaeology. He was a most interesting man.

We have established that the long climatic downturn led to the formation of peat over much of the surface of the islands. How quickly it formed, and how long it took before someone found out that you could dry and burn the peat, as I was doing thousands of years later, is, as far as I am concerned, anyone's guess. But at some stage this became commonplace, and led to a new social and cooking arrangement, the physical manifestation of which has become known as the Burnt Mound.

The mound itself is the most conspicuous element of the site. When dug into it was found to consist largely of broken or shattered bits of stone that had clearly been heated – plus all sorts of other bits of contemporary rubbish of much interest to archaeologists, smashed pottery or bits of bone. Such heaps adjoin, often almost encircle, the remains of a building, the most significant elements of which are usually a hearth and a large stone tank set into the floor. It is generally agreed, I think, that these elements were part of a cooking process, by which peat was burned on the hearth, stones were placed in the fire till they were hot and then shuffled somehow over to the tank of water and pushed in. Eventually, the temperature rose enough for a joint of meat to be cooked in it. This has been done experimentally, just to prove that it works. In this process, the heated stone tends to shatter in the cold water, and so at the end of the cooking, there is a fair amount of debris to be collected up – generally, as far as one can see, chucked out of the door, to accumulate slowly in the following decades or even centuries. This would have one, incidental, benefit – that of providing a little shelter to the door of the structure. I deliberately use the word "structure" in this context because these were not houses. Very few of them have actually been excavated (hence the importance of Liddle), but in general there seem to be no beds within the building. These must have been communal eating places; in other words, to be facetious perhaps, the first restaurants (what was I saying earlier about civilisation moving south?).

It is often pointed out that this whole arrangement could also have been used as a bath-house of some kind; one can only concede that in the contemporary climate a luxury like this would have been most welcome. Such mounds, presumably mostly with associated but less visible structures, occur right down the western side of Britain. This means, it seems to me, that Liddle must be as significant to Bronze Age Britain as Skara Brae is to Neolithic Europe; another great treasure of our archaeology, perhaps still somewhat under-valued. The area of blown sand in Westray known as the Links of Noltland seems to contain a similar but significantly more elaborate development of the same idea, a structure not yet fully understood and without parallel in the islands or further afield. This part of the island, where erosion by wind and rabbits is powerful and ongoing, may well prove to contain enormous archaeological riches – if the sea does not claim them before we see them.

As a discipline, archaeology has had an unfortunate tendency to be dominated by the evolution of fashionable ideas, which have sometimes involved the vigorous rubbishing of previously held notions. For quite a long time, it was held that this succession of archaeological ages, the Stone, Bronze and Iron Ages (and so on), necessarily involved the immigration of, or invasion by, new groups and cultures from Europe or perhaps even further afield. Then, for a period, these ideas became rather discredited, and spontaneous local development was the fashionable theory – somewhat overstated, in my view. I could never see why it could be postulated that people in prehistory were presumed not to have moved into other countries, not to have invaded other cultures, when we know well that this certainly happened in history: the example of the invading Norsemen and Normans, for instance, must go unchallenged. Now, however, DNA studies, fashionable in themselves, have rather come to the rescue of the traditional view.

Recent reports of work done by geneticists from Trinity College, Dublin, and archaeologists from Queen's University, Belfast, show that "early Irish farmers (Neolithic) were similar to southern Europeans", and that "Genetic patterns then changed dramatically in the Bronze Age, as newcomers from the eastern periphery of Europe settled in the Atlantic region" (published in the journal *PNAS*). The geneticist who led the study, Professor Dan Bradley, added: "This degree of genetic change invites the possibility of other associated changes, perhaps even the introduction of language ancestral to western Celtic tongues."

This at least encourages me that I may still write that the next architectural developments in the north of what we now call Scotland (and in Orkney) are due to the arrival, perhaps before 500 BC, of Celtic people from Europe, the first group for which we have a straightforward name. This is the beginning of the Iron Age in the islands, and that the structures dating from this period are as impressive as any from the previous ages.

Eight

Along the Evie Shore

On the occasion of my first solo trip to Orkney, I camped, most nights, behind the Evie Sands. There was a considerable amount of open space here that no one else seemed to be using for any purpose, as well as a handy public loo at the northwestern end of the beach, where the side-road comes down from Evie village. To this day, there are loos there (splendid ones, too) and a car park, and down on the shore you may see, part-buried by sand, a small stone pier. I have not seen the pier being used for decades, although I guess it may be in use in high summer, but at that time, a boat ran across to Frotoft in Rousay, and I recall being down there one evening as it was being loaded with people and shopping. A similar small pier, its opposite number as it were, can still be seen on the Rousay coast.

The parking space was often the starting point for a walk along the Evie shore, going just as far northwest as we felt inclined. On the map, this is almost a straight line, but when walking it, it feels like a series of very shallow bays, with flat rocks running out into the Sound of Eynhallow at regular intervals. It was very much a walk for good days, and somewhat dependent on the state of the tide, as the ungrazed vegetation of the narrow strip of land between the beach and the fences of the long, down-sloping fields, tended to be dense and tall, obscuring a number of rabbit holes. You also had to be careful on the slabs of sandstone – if they were damp, they could be quite slippery, and if covered with a greenish growth, were liable to be lethal. (This applies all over Orkney: be careful if the rocks are wet.)

The same shallow bays could also hold a few traps for the unwary, as in places the winter gales had deposited a considerable depth of chopped-up, half-rotted seaweed, which could be remarkably glutinous, and sometimes smelled quite strongly, too. These patches of weed tended to be full of sandflies, which might be slightly annoying to us, but they lured a number of birds, including busy parties of iridescent starlings.

But, despite the possible hazards, it was a lovely walk, sometimes on dry slabs (many marked clearly with ripples and mud-cracks), sometimes on sand. In front of us were the shallow, aquamarine waters of the Sound of Eynhallow, and across it, the long, dark ridge of Rousay. It was a walk for a morning or an afternoon, a gentle stroll looking for birds or seals, or simply marvelling at the beauty of the isles.

There always seemed to be something to look at, and parties of birds moved away from the shore as we walked along. Frequently these were female eider with ducklings, always fun to watch as they bob and scuttle about on the water, or female shelduck, with their crèches of youngsters, perhaps well over a dozen of them in the early summer. The red-throated divers flew down from their lochans in the moors, where they bred, and sometimes landed immediately in front of us, showing the rich cinnamon colour that gives them their name. They give a harsh cackle as they fly, so we knew when to watch out for them, and on occasion they presented us with an amazing display. Once three of them took part, but as there is effectively no difference between the sexes we were not always entirely certain of the dynamics within the group. Presumably it would be two rival males displaying to one female. For most of the time, two of them were certainly running up and down on the surface of the water, necks outstretched, wings out to the side, all three continually uttering their unearthly calls.

This shore was good for waders, and if we walked quietly and slowly, we would have excellent views. Depending exactly when we were there, we frequently saw turnstones, which would later move yet further north to breed. There were normally several of the smaller waders, slightly solemn, the masked ringed plover and black-bellied dunlin. Oystercatchers were ubiquitous, and often a great nuisance, as they would create a fiendish racket as soon as they saw us, alerting every other bird to our presence. Redshank were common, while the daily fly-past would include cormorants and shags, Arctic terns and the occasional, dramatic-looking sandwich tern, visiting kitti-wakes or fast-flying squadron of auks. But we were watching for the skuas, of course, and they seldom failed to materialise. The Arctics often hunted in pairs, while the bigger, blunter bonxies were usu-ally alone. We saw one trying very hard to pluck ducklings from the surface of the water. They were desperately diving and scuttling in all directions, but in the end the skua was successful, and carried one off – only to be mobbed itself by great black-backed gulls. On another occasion, we saw the great skua's tactics for catching terns, especially young ones. It simply flew straight at them, crashing into them so that they fell in a flailing heap to the water. Down came the skua after it, and held it under the water until it had drowned. I was always hoping that these dramas would not take place just as we were sitting calmly on some rocks in the sun, enjoying a quiet lunch, as it could be quite upsetting to watch this entirely natural behaviour at close quarters. Nor was the sight of a neat, clean, entirely inoffensive brown rat very popular among the guests.

One of the aims of this walk was to get good sightings of seals, and we were seldom disappointed. Sometimes an individual common seal, calm and inquisitive like a pet dog, nosed in and out of the little bays, really close to us if we stayed quiet. Often, there would be many more hauled out on some slabs, and if I could get my group in place without alarming them, we could spend an age, watching them dozing, scratching, waving a flipper in the air, snoring and farting. Once or twice this flatulence gave rise to one of those impossible occasions when an entire group of people suddenly gets the giggles, and attempts to stifle them only make the situation worse, until everyone is quite hysterical with laughter. There were normally a few grey or Atlantic seals in among all the common, and we spent some lovely hours just watching such groups.

One rather hazy day sticks in my mind. We were sitting on a low bank having lunch, listening to the distant, eerie calls of the divers, watching the translucent water softly wash the sand, when a solitary fulmar, dark-eyed and solemn, glided past on its stiff wings, almost touching the surface of the sea. It appeared rather intrigued by our quiet, appreciative group, and turned, repeating the performance several times, coming closer on each fly-past, calm and inscrutable.

By this time, we were quite far along the coast, opposite the low island that gives the Sound its name. Eynhallow means the Holy Island, and it has been suggested that its name comes from the presence of what is generally believed to be a small, unrecorded monastery of the twelfth century. From where we were sitting, we could see the buttresses that support the walls of the church, and it did indeed look very peaceful in the soft, azure light. Another fact about this small isle does concern fulmars: it was here that a long-running investigation into these birds by a team from the University of Aberdeen discovered that they are very long-lived. One, named George in honour of the professor who led the study, George Dunnett, was eventually found to be over 50 years old. Among their many fascinating characteristics, fulmars have complete mastery of the air, and gave us many hours of pleasure simply watching their aerial skills.

Above the low bank behind the beach were the fields, and sometimes they were worth watching, too. As well as a few brown hares to be seen, on more than one occasion a harrier would come down low over the grass to check out the shore. Sometimes it flew directly over our heads, which was a great thrill. The furthest I ever remember reaching on this walk was the ruin of a chambered cairn at the Point of Hisber. By this time we had passed three unploughed mounds, also archaeological sites, two of them at least endowed with the name "Knowe". I am never sure in what way a "knowe" may differ from a "howe", but both words mean "mound". All three on the way out to Hisber were believed to be the site of brochs; at least one certainly was, possessing a good section of high curved wall.

The broch is perhaps the "classic" monument of Iron Age Celtic Scotland, and, once back at the loos and car park, if you look to the other end of the great sweep of sand, the far, low headland is the location of one of these splendid structures. This is the Broch of Gurness, for me the most wonderful of all the roll-call of Orkney sites. For once, perhaps, "iconic" is the appropriate word. I suppose it is the combination of the location – one of the most beautiful in the islands – the scale and strength of the remains, and the aura of romance that I can still weave around this site from some imagined Heroic Celtic Age. (This all started during my childhood with visits to the imposing Clachtoll Broch in Assynt and a vague acquaintance with some of the Irish myths.) It also happens to be a place where the beauties of the wild and natural world combine with the ancient and man-made. I have so often had to break off an archaeological commentary to watch, close-up, enchanting groups of eider or divers, a sudden frenzy of diving terns, or the fun of passing, "porpoising" common seals.

This extensive site was once simply a rounded grassy hill, with a scattering of stones over it, when Robert Rendall, a multi-talented man (one of whose poems we have already met), set up his easel in order to paint the view across to Rousay. The story goes that one of the legs of his easel went down into a rabbit hole, and when on his knees to extricate it, he decided that what he was seeing was actually part of a wall, some of which he subsequently uncovered. During the later excavation of the whole, enormous site, the decision was taken to uplift the most recent structures, the first uncovered, and to re-erect them to one side of the main monument, the broch and its surrounding housing behind the strong ramparts. Deciding how to excavate a monument, and then to present it to public view, involves very difficult decisions and many compromises, but the result at Gurness makes a genuine impact on many of its visitors. It is a pity only that the endearing little museum/ticket office/shop should have been erected so close to the excavated buildings. It would be wonderful if it might one day be relocated to the wide car park where it would lie lower and be less conspicuous, as well as more sheltered.

At one point, there was a tendency in archaeological circles to downplay the defensive qualities of the broch (the most complete of which, the astonishing Broch of Mousa, is in Shetland). But an examination of Gurness, with its complex external ramparts and central tower, makes it reasonably clear that when constructed (presumably some time after 500 BC), there was a real need for defence from some perceived enemy. Who that enemy might have been we do not know. It is not yet easy to estimate how tall these individual towers may have been, but there seems to be a general agreement that few would have equalled Mousa, which survives to some forty-five feet all round. Experiments by John Barber (already mentioned), in constructing and then collapsing broch walls, enable us to understand rather better the unexcavated ruins with their great spreads of fallen stone. (One of the most significant of these is, in fact, Clachtoll, and recent work of clearance and excavation has given a much better idea of the scale of the surviving monument.) But the tower itself, of whatever height, with its thick, double-skinned walls and featureless exterior, has an undoubted defensive quality. Like many a mediaeval castle, its powerful presence combines the practical, protective and prestigious aspects that denote the residence of a powerful individual. The entrance, the one weak point, is afforded extra protection at many of these Orcadian sites (and probably also at Clachtoll), by a forward-projecting structure with an outer doorway, which is likely to have housed some guard dogs.

Like Gurness, Clachtoll has further external protection, and there appear to be a few structures, presumably houses, in the open space between the broch and the outer rampart. But the housing and the ramparts at Gurness are on a far greater scale, and it seems that some of the presumably later and larger houses are actually built out into the first of the big ditches between the walls. I take this to indicate that defensive needs had by this time been relaxed. It would appear that a very significant area of the site has been lost to the erosive power of the sea, so its original extent is simply guesswork, but the scale of each house within the community may easily be seen. They are divided by splendid slab walls, and each is provided with a hearth, a stone tank for cooking (just as in the Bronze Age), some stone beds, possibly bunk-style, and little cupboards in the walls. Similar details may be seen in the courtyard of the broch itself. In one of the houses there is a rather larger stone fitting, which I believe was intended to be watertight, and which may even have been a bath.

Many of the Orkney sites labelled "broch" show a large mound, presumably representing the remains of a similar tower, often surrounded by an unploughed area of ground. These would have remained unploughed simply because of the amount of stone they contained; many of them must therefore be like Gurness: a fortified community around a stronghold. Some are in spectacular, and notably defensive, locations. Two are somewhat similar in position and the scale of the surrounding structures, but offer visitors a very different experience. Midhowe on Rousay, close to the great tomb, was excavated by Walter Grant, later stabilised and taken into state guardianship. On the other hand, the Broch of Borwick on the coast north of Yesnaby, rather smaller than Midhowe, was excavated at the instigation of William Watt of Skaill in 1881. It has since been left to the mercy of the elements and of humanity, which, one way or another, has much reduced its structure. It is, however, a wonderful place, situated like Midhowe between two impressive geos. (This word "geo" is common, despite variations in pronunciation and spelling, all around the Scottish coast – and therefore presumably Norse in origin – and refers to a narrow, quite often almost straight-sided inlet between cliffs.) It is obvious, when visiting either site, that the towers experienced structural problems, possibly because of inadequate foundations, and that parts of the circular walls of both eventually collapsed. At Midhowe, this reveals part of the "gallery" within the double-skinned, immensely thick walls. Such a feature acted effectively as an internal scaffolding, enabling the builders to construct their high walls from within. This was useful in locations where tall, straight trees were non-existent, and when building close to the edge of cliffs. Only Midhowe gives us a glimpse of the technological skill of the builders, using long stones as tie-beams across structural voids in order to preserve structural integrity and strength while reducing weight, as in the lintels necessary to bridge the entrance passages. (Such details are best seen at Dun Carloway in Lewis, the twin brochs in Glen Beag by Glenelg, and, of course, in the extraordinary tower of Mousa.) Because there are very few variations in the broch plans, it is often conjectured that there was at this time a class of master-mason or architect who could understand and organise the building of these sophisticated monuments.

The reader may have noticed that, once again, our ancestors were able to undertake the planning and construction of impressive projects during this period. It seems that the long climatic downturn had by now at least flattened out, or the weather might actually have been improving. In addition, the use of iron-tipped ploughs, perhaps pulled by oxen, is likely to have allowed the cultivation of heavier ground than ever before. In a place like Orkney, maybe almost everywhere at this time, the climate, and its interaction with the soil, placed obvious limits on people's lives. But when they could, they displayed remarkable powers of visualisation, organisation and construction. The beauty of the settings of these monuments is an added bonus – but perhaps their builders were conscious of this, too.

Nine

Iron Age Enigmas

Were we in the astonishingly unlikely position of excavating all the lumps and bumps that have been labelled as brochs on the maps, we would probably find that not all of them conform to the pattern of Gurness, Midhowe or Borwick. While a number might turn out to have very thick walls, we can anticipate that others would lack the specialised features regarded as necessary for any building to qualify as a broch. This is a discussion of which I am very wary, as Scottish archaeology has tended to get its collective knickers in a twist when confronted with the problem of categorising and naming the full range of circular structures adorning our countryside. Neolithic houses in Orkney, when found in villages such as Skara Brae, are very roughly square with rounded corners; individual houses, as sometimes seen in Shetland, seem to be more oval, and so have, mercifully, avoided the use of the term "roundhouse". The circular houses of the Bronze Age languished for a long time under the somewhat pejorative description of "hut circle". However, these have since been accorded the rather more dignified title of "Bronze Age roundhouses", while those of the subsequent period, instead of simply being referred to as "Iron Age roundhouses", which would be both logical and easy to comprehend, have become "Atlantic roundhouses". Within this classification, there seems to be an almost infinite gradation of "brochness" (to coin a term!), and it now rather depends on which author you pick, as to how the relevant monument is described. In this context, for instance, I have often wondered whether the impressive structure on its island outside Lerwick, always referred to as the "Broch of Clickhimin", would actually now be accorded that description. And in the Northern Isles, the term "dun", frequently applied elsewhere to a thick-walled, circular structure, is never used. What all this means is that there exist other buildings of the Iron Age, in Orkney and elsewhere, that may well be older, but which may foreshadow, in one way or another, the construction of the imposing broch towers. Sadly, there is remarkably little of them for the average visitor to see.

Within the archipelago there may be some sort of sequence: from the relatively thin-walled roundhouse excavated at Quanterness (perhaps dating to about 700 BC); through that at Bu (outside Stromness), which initially had a wall of more than four feet that was later augmented to just around sixteen; to the extraordinary efforts at nearby Howe farm. Here, among other things, there was once a fine chambered tomb, which survived into the Iron Age, when it was converted into what we presume was an underground storage chamber and seems to have been capped with clay. On top of this, a large roundhouse was then constructed, but it was probably provided with inadequate foundations and subsequently collapsed. There then followed, with dogged determination, an effort to build not one but two broch-like structures. The second was simpler than the first attempt and may have lasted longer; it was surrounded by contemporary houses and a new set of ramparts. I well remember being shown round this astonishing site by John Hedges and Beverly Ballin Smith. In passing, it is worth mentioning that the roundhouse at Quanterness was set into part of the conspicuous green mound that may still be seen on site. This contained a tomb, access to whose chamber may have remained open.

One last point in connection with the incredible site of Howe is that nothing of it remains, and I recall being told that the physical remnants of the structures simply became incorporated into the farm tracks. At the time, I lamented the fact that this was allowed to happen, although I have to admit that no one, faced with the mound that had stood there, could have guessed at what it contained (shades of Midhowe cairn!). Nor, I dare say, could they have found a way to access the funds required to leave any of it in place, even if the farmer were willing for this to happen. But even a segment of the excavated mound would have been hugely impressive, as well as of the greatest educational value. It has been claimed that this site was as important as Jarlshof in Shetland. We must be careful that we do not destroy others of similar significance.

My beloved volume *The Northern Isles*, edited by F.T. Wainwright, pointed out a number of probable "pre-broch" structures, at Howmae in North Ronaldsay, on the Calf of Eday and at the Little Howe of Hoxa, on the Scapa Flow coast of South Ronaldsay; others have been investigated since. The Little Howe was excavated by George Petrie, and found to have a gallery within the thick walls, a feature that might place it among the broch prototypes. Sadly, when I last visited it, it was not in a good state. Bits of the wall looked close to collapse, it seemed there had been a few "casual and informal" attempts to dig into it, and it appeared as though animals had been trampling over the site. Although I fully recognise that the almost endless range of archaeological sites within Orkney makes it hard to decide where and how the limited funding should be used, we do have a responsibility to respect the monuments of the past, and an obligation not just to watch their remains disappear.

Comparatively little attention has been paid to a whole category of sites that presumably date from the Iron Age; as a result, we know little of their relationship to the brochs and the surrounding communities. I am thinking of the various promontory forts. Some sites that might qualify under this description include the Brough of Deerness and possibly even the Brough of Birsay. These were subsequently occupied by the Norse, so they should really be considered as belonging to a later culture. The headland known as the Brough of Bigging at Yesnaby is one which I frequently walk by, or on to, and ponder over. The use of the term "brough" for such sites suggests that for some time people have recognised a common feature: the fact that a simple wall across the narrow neck of a cliff-girt headland rapidly provides you with a site that it is easy to defend. Here at the Brough of Bigging there appear to be two possible defences: the first a bank behind a natural gully that may have been deepened, and the second a line of stones across the narrowest neck of the promontory – although details here may be confused with, or by, a local story that drowned sailors were sometimes buried near here. Be that as it may, on the top of the headland (which gives wonderful coastal views), a few vertical slabs indicate fairly clearly the remains of some sort of structure. There are other such places around the coast but how they actually functioned is not necessarily very clear. Were they simply moderately safe places to keep stock when raiders threatened, or were they in fact occupied by a human population, even if only at times of stress?

Such questions come to the fore in one of the most unlikely places imaginable. When I used to walk the high ground of the very west of Hoy, I had a healthy tendency to keep some distance away from the edge of the magnificent cliffs, which are much better seen from the ferry than from above. The culmination of these cliffs is the impressive St John's Head, part of which is almost detached from the great precipice and bears the significant name of Bre Brough. You can (though I never did!) "cross a narrow saddle and climb a series of ledges". Further up, a narrow approach is blocked by a short stone wall, and above this there is a significant, broad turf bank.

This information comes from the Orkney Sites and Monuments Register, and was written by Raymond Lamb, whom I knew well, and who earns my respect for making the crossing to investigate this awe-inspiring location (as well as for the huge amount of fieldwork he undertook in the islands when he was County Archaeologist). Somewhat naturally, this site has had little, if any, further investigation, so we remain in the dark as to how this improbable location was used.

There is yet another class of monument, possibly used in the Iron Age and still comparatively unexplored. These are frequently referred to as "crannogs", to my mind another unhelpful term as it indicates only that the site is an artificial (or modified) island. There are several such sites, the most obvious of which can be seen in the loch of Wasbister in Rousay, and close to Voy, on the shore of the large loch of Stenness. Some of these are almost circular; when the water is low, causeways leading out to the two at Voy are visible.

However vague we may be about some aspects of Iron Age Orkney, one type of structure – frequently but not always associated with the brochs – seems, counter-intuitively, to be becoming more enigmatic as time passes. When I first visited Orkney and spent ages marvelling at Gurness, there was a very visible feature in the broch's courtyard, which we all, quite sensibly, called a well. Brochs are defensive, residential structures in which people would live, and a water supply would be of obvious benefit. The well in the courtyard at Gurness is now very difficult to appreciate, protected as it is by a rather emphatic grille. I recall, however, that it was neatly built, with carefully constructed stone walls, and steps that led down into the well chamber. As we had been looking around the whole site, the careful construction did not seem in the least bit odd to us, simply an indication of the usual care taken by the builders of Orkney's high-status Iron Age sites. As to the steps, they appeared, and seem to me today, to be very sensible. Water levels in wells tend to fluctuate, and the steps allowed anyone collecting water to descend a little bit further to collect the water when it was at a lower level. I never remember anyone quibbling with this idea. Other strongholds also had wells within their bounds: Midhowe Broch, the Brough of Deerness and Cubbie Roo's Castle on Wyre. It all appeared to make sense.

One site in particular has led many to challenge this simple explanation. It is one that in itself seems to make absolutely no sense at all: Mine Howe, in the East Mainland. Almost everything about this building defies logic. Its mound is one of a number of small mounds located around a larger, longer one called Long Howe, and as far as I can tell, they are all assumed at the moment to be natural – a very dangerous assumption in Orkney! This area was certainly considered significant during the Bronze and Iron Ages. There are many signs of Iron Age activity in the immediate neighbourhood, but the two most obvious mounds, in terms of physical remains, are, to say the least, enigmatic. The road crosses through one of them, a roughly circular feature; from the air it looks quite large and somewhat mucked about with – and possibly too narrow in the wall to conform to the pattern of Gurness or Midhowe. If it had any sort of defensive purpose, surely it would have been built on the relative eminence of Long Howe, not tucked under its end? It lies on flat ground, which, according to most commentators, would have been marshland at the time, suggesting that water levels at that date would have been higher than they are now (this is a crucial point). Because of these factors, I incline to caution when describing it. Some kind of roundhouse, perhaps? Or just an enclosure?

But it gets worse. The problem is Mine Howe itself. The site basically consists of a mound, which was once surrounded by a ditch. This, of course, leads everyone to think of the Neolithic – if it had a chamber, is it another Maeshowe? If solid and, apparently, without any structure, another Silbury Hill? So far so good, but the site has obstinately refused to produce anything of any Neolithic significance, and it was clearly the centre of considerable later activity, including much metalworking. So what have we actually got? What is unarguable, I think, is that there is a natural mound. During the Iron Age the locals got the notion of digging out a large shaft in its middle, probably right down to bedrock, as there are slabs of sandstone at the bottom. Within that shaft they then constructed a stair-tower, all the way up to the top of the mound. They must then have filled in the gap between the tower and the sides of the mound. Immediately, this raises questions: what did the cross-section of the tower look like? What about its external walls? Answering these questions may be necessary before hazarding a guess as to the role of the site. Also, why, having sunk the shaft and constructed the tower, did they not just fill in the gaps with material from the (remaining) crest of the mound, requiring less building and creating a level area on its summit at the same time? Was it important to maintain both the height and profile of the mound, and, if so, why? Most obvious of all, why go to all the bother anyway?

At the bottom of the flight of stone stairs there is something of a drop, and this has led folk to suggest that the resultant, shallow, stone-walled pit may have functioned as a well. There is no "piping in", however, as far as I can see, to lead in the waters from a captured spring. Nor are there any signs of a "tideline", which might indicate any long-term water level – although one would have to admit that such a mark might not survive the passage of time, plus two emptyings of the accumulated contents of the shaft. But it is worth noting that if it were once a well, the space down there is so limited that it would be possible only for someone to descend to the bottom of the steps, stop at the water, turn around, and start back up again.

As a ritual space, even for one person, it is awkward and limited. The same applies, incidentally, to the well in the Gurness courtyard, whose purpose is now also questioned. Supposing it did function as a well, pure, simple and utilitarian, or a well with ritual significance, why, for goodness' sake, decide to reach the water level from one of the highest available points? And if the water level here were higher than it obviously is now (the "well" being dry), how tenable would life at the other end of Long Howe be, in a roundhouse in the swamp?

If the water level were high enough to fill the well, building the lower courses of the walls of the stair-tower must have been rather awkward, and the site constricted within the limits of the excavated shaft. One thing that has struck me quite forcibly is that contrary to the comments of a number of people, this building is not constructed of fine masonry. For a presumably high-status site of the Orcadian Iron Age, it is actually quite crude, but what one should deduce from this, I am not sure. I do know that the two "galleries" that lead from the turn in the "U"-shaped stair have added to the ritualistic atmosphere of the place – I recall reading about consulting oracles and so on. Given the problems of building an unmortared stair-tower in a narrow shaft, and the very unequal stresses on the central wall of the "U", my guess is that the "galleries", which are on the (otherwise) unsupported side of the stair, represent building platforms and buttressing for the centre of the structure. These were then roofed over, perhaps for storage of some kind.

I read, too, of an ongoing excavation at the Cairns, in South Ronaldsay; what was thought initially to be a well was subsequently revealed to be a souterrain under the broch courtyard. This takes me back to Howe, where the original chambered tomb was later converted, effectively, into a souterrain under the floor of the succession of massive structures, However, as I recall, only a child or contortionist could have managed to enter it. When the souter-rains were called "earth-houses", they too, were enigmatic, as it was hard to work out how anyone might actually live in them. Then they emerged – quite sensibly, as far as I am concerned – as storage places for items you needed to keep cool, meat and dairy produce. Wells, too, were practical requirements, neatly constructed in the Orkney manner. But now, all thanks to the impossibility that is Mine Howe, both are linked and are acquiring, year by year, more and more layers of conjecture, more constant use of the dreaded word "ritual". In their *Caithness Archaeology*, Andy Heald and John Barber include a short chapter on "Wells". They adopt, mercifully, a very measured tone in discussing precisely the same vexed question from a Caithness viewpoint. However, they leave me, as does all the foregoing discussion, with a burning question, one of simple logic: *Should we be reviewing the practical probabilities of many souterrains and broch wells, in the light of the construction of a single stair-tower within a natural mound, whose purpose is still completely incomprehensible to us?*

Ten

Boat Trips

In the previous chapters I have mentioned many of the natural facets of the Orkney landscape. A few, such as the native sandstone, we have discussed at some length as being a major resource for the inhabitants of the archipelago. That type of resource, and its use, is obvious even to us today. But for many who live in the urban concentrations of the twenty-first century, others, for instance those that may be gathered on the shore, are less self-evident. In fact, a consideration of the resources available to past inhabitants of the islands does suggest that while the climate of their home might impose real restrictions on them, the natural resources available could fairly be described as generous.

We have seen that since Neolithic times, the Orcadians were farmers. They brought with them crops and stock, both of which could help feed them. But they found a group of islands populated with game birds (although grouse are not exactly a common species today) and animals. Or at least they *probably* did – although red deer bone and antler are common in the local archaeological record, for instance, there is nothing, as far as I am aware, to indicate that red deer carcasses might not have been imported from the Highlands. That is just an idea, perhaps a little fanciful, but the implications of a local red deer population and agriculture do have to be considered. In my previous book (*Castles in the Mist*, Saraband, 2016) I indicated that in the Highlands, because of the considerable and scattered rural population that depended on growing crops, the red deer must have been limited to core areas, and the population kept under some control. The big deer drives occasionally referred to, and testified by archaeological remains in places like Rum, must have achieved this. In Orkney, however, we know that many more islands than at present were populated and must have been farmed. Wild, hilly country is scarce, and distances between islands are not great (and red deer are surprisingly powerful swimmers), so the idea of deer and agriculture coexisting is actually a difficult one. The only real possibility would lie in creating "reserves", and we do know that impressive walls or dykes might have been so used. The very thick wall across the headland at Brodgar was made of stone, but others, such as the "treb" dykes in some islands, were mostly turf. It is just possible that these might have been built up high enough to keep deer from leaping over – although they could still, obviously, have swum around the ends.

With other natural resources, we may be rather more confident. The great seabird colonies would have represented food to earlier populations – and a lot of it. Perhaps the best-known rural economy with a huge reliance on the bird cliffs is that of St Kilda. As that community survived until quite recently and has been well described and illustrated, it is easy to imagine the same sort of vertiginous activity transferred to Noup Head or Marwick. Going down over the cliff edge on a rope to gather eggs or young birds, always a risky activity, could have brought immense dividends as far as the daily diet was concerned (and other practical benefits such as supplies of natural oil) – if you survived.

The men of Ness, in Lewis, also still take their harvest of the "gugas", so we can gain some sense of the life of the cliffs, an aspect that now tends to be forgotten. Fishing off the rocks or lower cliffs was commonplace, but in recent years the only location where I have seen it still enthusiastically practised has been on the rugged Catalonian coast of southern France! I did once find an easy way down into the lower cliffs that march up from Birsay Bay to the crest of Marwick Head. It would have been feasible to fish in quite deep water from there or, perhaps, to investigate some of the bird ledges from below – maybe with a long rod and noose arrangement, as they did in St Kilda. I visited it only for short periods of quiet contemplation, and some illicit sunbathing!

Many birds are to be found around the lochs, too, and in the winter there is – and presumably always was – an enormous population of overwintering geese and duck, especially on the wide waters of Scapa Flow. Both the sea and the lochs contain fish, and it is not long since significant numbers of boats made use of the few good landing places on the more exposed coasts. I have already mentioned the fishermen's huts at Sand Geo, where a channel, cleared of boulders, used to be nearly always visible. At some stages of the tide it still is, but the whole beach is now covered with stones, and hauling a boat up there would be very difficult. Boats continue to use a small, sandy inlet of Birsay Bay, under the headland of Buckquoy. Not far around that attractive coast, at Skippiegeo, a group of little boat-shaped nousts, in whose comparative shelter small- to medium-sized boats would be left, may still be seen. Going fishing, whether on the sea or the lochs, is still a major Orcadian activity. Nowadays I assume that much of the catch is frozen, but when I was living there, it was still quite common to see filleted fish hung out on a line to dry, the "stockfish" of the old days.

Apart from offering the possibility of shellfish (and even seaweed), with the occasional stranded whale, the shores could provide seals, although they were presumably more wary in the past than they are now. Locations like Hisber or Birsay Bay, where seals are now so common, may once have been rather quieter, but boats would have helped in the hunt. It is such a shame that we are so short here of ancient boats, and cannot be confident how they were made in the earliest periods at which we have been looking.

Unlike some of my immediate forebears, and most unlike several of those more distant, I am far from being a practical sailor, although I love being on the water (in it, too, in warmer climes), and cope happily with quite rough seas. Being so close to the ocean in Birsay, I acquired a huge respect for the sea, and did not exactly rush to get out into the complex tides and currents that swirl around the islands. But we did make a few autumnal charters in order to get close to the grey seal, which breeds in the autumn and must have been a considerable resource for the ancient inhabitants. We did this, I hasten to say, only on calm days, the "day between weathers" that is so special during the autumnal gales. There were a few occasions when the sea was glassy calm, and motoring along quietly between low headlands had a hypnotic quality; once or twice a heavy swell made landing impossible, but these few days were always special.

We used to hire a fine motor-yacht, whose owner and skipper (assisted sometimes by his son) was a splendid man, a pleasant and, I think, very strong character. We joined them in Kirkwall, sailing out into the bay, and soon into the expanse of Wide Firth, with a misty Rendall on one side and Shapinsay on the other. Once, we circumnavigated the small island of Gairsay, with its conspicuous heather hill, and the fine old house of Langskaill. A few auks bobbed alongside us, the odd fulmar swept by on imperious wings as we passed the low shapes of Wyre and Egilsay. Our destination was always a pair of smaller isles or holms: Muckle Green Holm and Little Green Holm were the names on the map (although everyone used "Peedie" for the latter, the traditional Orcadian word for little). Here the grey seals haul out to breed, squabble and mate. As we approached Muckle Green Holm there were many seals in the water around us, and we quietly landed at the south end, before making our cautious way to where we could overlook the north part of the grassy islet. There was a scene of splendid chaos, with some seals basking, some making their inelegant way to or from the water and some mothers quietly suckling. We counted perhaps eighty pups, a few as much as two weeks old and already quite feisty – which they needed to be, amid the heaving, massive bodies of the adult bulls.

There were also quite a few birds on the holms. On the larger of the two were a number of wigeon with lots of greylag geese off Shapinsay, both of which we had anticipated. Less appropriate, however, on these flat, open, grassy expanses, were two goldcrests, of which we had repeated, excellent views. Another day, the tide was running too fast for us to land on either of the two Green Holms. Instead we visited Helliar Holm, close in to Shapinsay, and the Holm of Scockness, which we reached after a lovely run up between the hills of Rousay and Egilsay, the low island dominated by the fine round tower of St Magnus' Church. We got very close to a large group of the smaller common seals here, and all along the shores there were big flocks of snipe. As the weather held, we decided the next day to head for Eynhallow, where we again got close to many common seals, including some of their pups, born in the calm weather of June and now quite large. There were two young Atlantic bulls in the water, and a great deal of rolling and splashing going on, but we thought it must all be in play, as there seemed to be no females near enough to inspire serious rivalry.

We also walked over the gentle slopes of the island to visit the old buildings presumed to belong to a twelfth-century monastery, of which there seems to be no written record. Although the church had been used latterly as a farmhouse, its round arch makes its original purpose and probable date quite clear. A number of gannets flew by, the black tips of their long wings emphasising the blinding white and yellowish head of these magnificent birds. There were also wigeon, mallard, eider and teal, and again great numbers of snipe, so, all in all, we had a magnificent day.

We frequently crossed from Stromness to Hoy, or from Tingwall to Rousay. Although the boats in those days were comparatively small, with room only for passengers, an amazing amount of stuff might be piled wherever there was room on deck – especially on the *Shalder*, the Rousay boat. I wrote about crossings when you might find yourself sitting on some bales of hay, or trying not to sit on the groceries for the small shop (in *North and West*, Scottish Cultural Press, 2003). The skipper of those days, Mansie Flaws, was a wonderful man, and in the course of many trips I got to know him very well. He was friendly, kind and helpful (and possessed of a splendid sense of humour), and on one trip he really excelled himself. I was out for the day with a friend who had a great interest in archaeology and old buildings, and had expressed a desire to visit Wyre and Egilsay. The way the timetable worked we would have some time in both islands, but it was not quite certain that there would be long enough in Wyre for us to visit the monument known as Cubbie Roo's Castle and its adjacent chapel. I mentioned this to Mansie, and as he lived on the island, he said he had an old car at the pier and could run us up to the sites, giving us ample time to visit and walk back. To this we happily agreed, and relaxed on the crossing, first to Brinyan on Rousay, and then across to Wyre where Mansie tied up the *Shalder* and we all left the boat.

He walked over to an old half-rusted car and managed to open the passenger door and one in the rear – the vehicle was distinctly battered but it could still move. I was well aware that on these small islands, where there are no garages, there is also no MOT requirement, and that very old cars simply soldier on until they die. This was clearly one such. It did not worry me, but my friend Roberta was an American, and unused to such wild ways. When she realised the back seat of the vehicle was part-occupied by an anchor and an old lobster-pot, and that it all smelled of salt and fish, she hesitated at the open door, looking very reluctant to enter. I quickly shoved her in and shut the door. When Mansie got in and started the car, the engine was rough and the exhaust blowing, but we headed for the quite steep hill that leads up from the pier. Halfway up, the car coughed and spluttered and ground to a halt; it appeared that we had run out of petrol. So Mansie simply let her career back down the hill, swerved to a halt, took an outboard engine off a nearby boat, up-ended this, via a filler, into the car, and off we set again. I was not very optimistic of the car's progress up the hill, as the contents of the outboard engine's fuel tank were presumably two-stroke, which the car might not like – but we did, just, manage the ascent and were duly delivered close to our goal. This was one trip I think Roberta never forgot!

Nor, obviously, did I. I wrote it up immediately I got home, not in any precise way, simply an attempt to record how I was feeling:

"The perfect day for a boat-trip among small islands; all colours deep and clear. The rich green-and-blue of the sea, greens and fawns of the lower ground, the deep, rich brown of the heather hill on Rousay, around which imposing island we sailed. The isles (Wyre and Egilsay) are very small and fertile, with a nice little valley across each, and fascinating old buildings on each; old, grey, heavily-lichened stones. Each island lay quiet, 'some other Eden', pastoral Orkney in its essentials.

The buildings themselves are intriguing and raise many questions. St Magnus' Church in Egilsay, St Mary's Church and Cubbie Roo's Castle in Wyre, the latter church under the hill on which the castle sits, and presumably in some close relationship with it. The most intriguing part of the castle is the large cistern, rather than just a well, and the fact that apparently the inner of the external ramparts, at least, seems to contain much older stone, and the castle appears to be built on top of something else. Was there a broch here earlier? (Funny that I can find no mention of these obvious facts.) The churches might have been built by the one hand, except for the Egilsay tower, and the habit there of using large blocks on their side in the walls. Very hard to date these structures, the arched doorways are very simple."

Eleven

Picts and Vikings

One grey day during that first solo visit, I wanted to explore the tidal island of the Brough of Birsay, so I headed for the corner of the West Mainland that over a decade later I would call home. In great contrast to current conditions, the "road" out to the Point of Buckquoy was then a rough, potholed track, beginning just after the quaint shore cottage called "Zanzibar". Shortly after that, it heaved itself up over a low ridge, which on the landward side had lost some of the covering of vegetation and sand, revealing the remains of stone structures. I parked the car carefully out of the way of others and had a good slow look at the jumbled stones, eventually coming to the conclusion that I must be seeing the remains of a house or houses, but of what period I could not tell. The site was not marked on my map, nor could I at the time find anything to read about it, so it remained something of a mystery, carefully indicated at the end of the day with a red cross. It is still legible today on my cloth, O.S. one-inch publication of 1959. I did feel it was quite special, but could not have told you why.

During the next winter, I had some time to myself – not exactly a gap year, but at least a few months before I went to "work" in Germany (simply in order to improve my grasp of the language). It was a quiet, dry winter, and I took to visiting the archaeological sites (mostly hill-forts) of North Fife, where we were then living. By now I was becoming very keen on archaeology, made moderately precise notes in the field, and read avidly on the topic. It so happened that within what might be called our extended family, we had a much older "cousin" who shared my interest. (She was actually a member of the family into which my grandmother had married, tragically briefly, at the end of the First World War, and they had all stayed in contact.) This "cousin" was a member of what I regarded very much as a learned society, and a great friend of its then secretary, Audrey Henshall, herself a well-respected archaeologist. As I began to bombard my almost-relation with questions and theories, she consulted with Audrey, and they eventually decided I should be put forward for membership of the learned society. So it came about that around the time of my twenty-first birthday, I was elected a Fellow of the Society of Antiquaries of Scotland, entitled, among other things, to use the library and attend lectures.

This latter possibility sounded very beguiling, but as lectures were held in Edinburgh (and, on occasion, in Aberdeen), and I went to work first of all in Inverness, subsequently to live in Assynt, attending them was a rare luxury. I was, however, extraordinarily fortunate in that I managed to attend a lecture given on the excavation of precisely the houses I had noted at Buckquoy. This was given by Anna Ritchie, and was remarkable in two ways: the first, as far as I was concerned, was simply Anna's way of lecturing – calm, warm, rational, gentle but clear. I made up my mind that this was exactly how one should speak in public, and have tried to do so ever since. Secondly, the content, too, was special, and important. This was the first modern excavation of the houses of the Picts, a people about whom there had always seemed to be plenty of romantic speculation but rather little in the way of facts about how they lived. They were best known for their considerable artistic achievements, especially their fine carved stones, but some of the symbols sculpted on those monuments were (and have remained) enigmatic, to say the least. I did know then that they were not the builders of the brochs, but descended from the comparatively nameless Celts who were. This was an evening of revelation, and I was lucky to be there.

When I came to live in Birsay, and went to revisit the site, there was now a smooth new road, and nothing of any structures to be seen. The excavation had been done in order to allow the improvement of the road to be carried out. Although I understood the impossibility of presenting anything of the excavated houses (at least in situ), I felt their loss almost as personal, a feeling that never entirely died. Many years later, I was made the first, part-time, Director of the Council for Scottish Archaeology (a voluntary body, despite the formality of its name – it is now Archaeology Scotland). Thinking of Buckquoy (as the site had become known), and all the others that had been excavated but left unexplained at best, destroyed at worst, I proposed a scheme of Archaeological Site Markers to try to remedy the situation. My suggestion was that such sites should simply be marked, with a plaque on a standing slab, with the site name, a simple plan, a brief but careful indication of its significance and, if possible, a note of where more information might be gleaned. This latter point was, and is, very important, as the information about such sites as Buckquoy and Howe may appear only in relatively obscure, learned, expensive volumes. "My" Pictish houses were fortunate in being written up and well-illustrated in the lovely book that Anna and Graham Ritchie later wrote: *Scotland-Archaeology and Early History*, published by Thames and Hudson in 1981. My mother gave it to me for my birthday that year, and Graham and Anna signed it when they stayed with us shortly after. Such site markers would not need to be placed exactly on the location of the excavated remains, but close by, not in anyone's way. The site marker for Buckquoy then could be near the road, rather than in its middle; for Howe, beside that road rather than in the farm, and so on. Markers should be of a standard, countrywide design, I think, but they could be sponsored by local businesses and tourist boards. Apart from being generally educational, they would critically emphasise the importance of that environment in the past, and contribute to a cultural tourism where the quality of the experience is what counts.

Anna's Pictish houses or "farmsteads" were complex in shape, cellular in plan, suggesting perhaps that the spaces for everyday living such as storage, cooking and sleeping were now more separate than had been the case in previous ages. The latest of these houses was substantial, some 15.8 metres long internally, and according to Anna and Graham, "its maximum width in the main hall was about 6m". Some finds, one with an "ogam" inscription (rather like the later runes, a form of script using straight lines that was relatively easy to carve), one a painted quartzite pebble, allowed the firm identification of these structures as pertaining to the Picts. This enabled a roughly similar group of cellular structures lifted from the upper layers of the Gurness excavations to be recognised as contemporary. The latter are comparatively fragmentary, and may give the visitor a misleading impression of low, huddled buildings. In fact, their ceilings were probably quite lofty. Around the broch at Jarlshof in Shetland, the wheelhouses, a class of circular building that seems to be strangely absent from Orkney, are surprisingly dignified, and I remember being told that the later houses at Howe had ceilings almost nine feet above the floor.

Elsewhere, the Picts are known to have built forts, including the substantial remains at Burghead, whose impressive ramparts (much still evident) have an internal timber structure, always referred to as "timber-laced". Clatchard Craig near Newburgh in Fife, and Dundurn in Perthshire, both of which I visited in that winter of exploration, were similar, and there was probably another such stronghold at the magnificent site of Dunnottar. Perhaps surprisingly, especially in view of subsequent events, we appear to have nothing comparable in the whole of the Northern Isles – although, as I mentioned earlier, our understanding of the promontory forts is lamentably poor. The multi-vallate structure at Ness of Burgi in Shetland intrigues me, but it, like other "block-house" forts both in Skye and Shetland, is generally considered to be earlier, Iron Age rather than Pictish. Again, we appear to have no similar structures in Orkney.

The headland of Buckquoy is eroding fast, with an archaeological structure falling out of its edge adjacent to the new stone steps, which go down to the beach. On walking across the causeway to the Brough, inspection of the approaching coast reveals that the cliff under the guardianship "settlement" is actually concrete and that an unknowable section of that site has long since been lost to the power of the sea. To the left, part of the low cliff is quite brightly coloured, ochre-to-red, and this must be fairly recently eroded; the further section, on the other hand, is black, indicating that it has been like that for much longer. But these vague comparisons give us little idea of the actual length of time involved, or whether or not it was a tidal island at the time of the Picts. What we know for sure is that the prevailing winds come from the southwest, with a fetch of maybe thousands of unimpeded miles. We know too that huge gales are a regular feature of the Orcadian climate, and that the erosive power of the ocean is seen here at its most impressive, constantly widening the gap that the visitor now crosses.

We know that the Picts occupied the island, but most of what we can see today belongs to a later period. It is possible that there was an early chapel on the site, maybe even a graveyard, but both were reused. An imposing standing stone, complete with symbols, was found in pieces and a cast of it placed, somewhat arbitrarily, close to the wall of the later graveyard. It at least firmly indicates a Pictish presence. This large site was excavated over an extended period by a number of individuals, most of whom would have been described,

I guess, as "great characters". In 1981 a conference was held on the subject of the island and its significance, and the critical day on site was marked by blazing sunshine. We walked around, and sat about, in all the glory of an Orkney summer – and it was easy to forget the open and very exposed nature of the location. I have two special memories of that day, which I think are reasonably accurate in detail, although I may have embellished them a little with the passing of time. The first is of listening to Ralegh Radford, who had been in charge of the original excavations. He has been variously described as the last of the "gentlemen antiquarians" and a "romantic historian", so he might be thought an odd choice to excavate a site for which the historical references are almost nil. He was eighty-one that year, and he stood on one of the low walls of the cemetery, unsupported, eyes tight shut, one hand outflung, the other covering his brow, and he lectured; at length perhaps, but certainly with fluent vigour. Then we separated into groups and I guided mine around the site, after which, seeing that there were still small numbers of people moving around, I attached myself to a group of acolytes following the almost equally formidable Mrs Curle, who provided the second memorable occasion of the day. We were down below the graveyard, passing a roughly circular, flat stone set in the short turf, when Mrs Curle walked over to it, pointed with her stick, and instructed one of our number to lift it, which he did with great care. "That," she said, "is my well. I found it, and the wretched man never put it in the guide-book." One gathered that the "pax academica" has not always prevailed on this location of scholarly importance! At the time, I took her description of it as a well for granted, but having looked at it several times since, I realise there are a few problems with this identification. It is a very small pit, made of rounded stones from the beach, and it was in it, and around it, that Mrs Curle found lots of evidence for Pictish metalworking on site.

We have therefore established on archaeological grounds that these sites of Gurness, Buckquoy, Birsay and others were occupied by the people known as the Picts. We are now at a point where we move, with faltering steps, into what ought to be the limelight of history. But it is also a point obscured by a lack of primary sources, embellished with some myth, much speculation and some rather persistent old habits. These latter include a tendency to focus on either the Northern or the Western Isles, almost as if they were different planets rather than two, not very distant, groups of islands, and to forget, almost always, what might actually be happening on that part of the Mainland that actually lies between them.

As far as "history" goes, what do we actually know about the end of the Pictish period in the far North? Adomnan, successor to, and biographer of, St Columba recorded a visit by the latter to the court of the Pictish king in Inverness, where a "regulus" or "regional king" was to be found. Columba wanted to send a missionary to the islands, to do what he had been doing everywhere else, which was to spread the Christian Gospel, and he wanted the assistance of the local king. This is reckoned generally to be 565 AD, only two years after his arrival in Iona, suggesting that Orkney was firmly part of the world of which Columba knew. How much success he had in converting Orkney remains speculative – apart, perhaps, from one important place-name, to which we shall return. And in 682 AD, not that long after, Bridei, King of the Picts, mounted an attack on Orkney. Why?

It seems to me that there are two possibilities. One is that, rather late in the day, Orkney revealed secessionist tendencies and threatened, somehow, to leave the federal Pictish kingdom. There is certainly nothing in the archaeological record that suggests to me a surge of Orcadian nationalism, however. Indeed, there is little to suggest much other than continuing agriculture at this late stage. The only other feasible reason, I conjecture, is that by then the Vikings have been exploring the Northern Isles and showed signs of making them a permanent base for more widespread activity. The Viking raids, on Lindisfarne in 793 AD, and on Iona in 795 AD, have tended to provoke suggestions that it was around 800 that Viking settlers began to arrive in some numbers in Orkney, but there is every reason to believe that sea-farers would have explored the archipelagos well before that, and perhaps Bridei wanted to re-establish his hold on the island group closest to the mainland of what we now call Scotland.

This is mere speculation, but the presence of a number of place-names incorporating the mysterious word "papar" (which is always agreed, I think, to refer to clergy of the Celtic Church, perhaps located here as a result of Columba's mission) is not. There are references in the *Historia Norwegiae* to the "papae", and the crucial place-name element is found in Orkney, Shetland, Caithness, the Outer Hebrides, Skye and Rum. What actually happened to the people so described, and to the Picts who lived in the houses at Buckquoy or Gurness, for instance, is much debated. Even if, by some chance or pestilence, one island group might have found itself much reduced in population, it is beyond credibility that the whole of the Atlantic province should be thus devastated. If all the papar had been slain during raids on their church property, it seems rather strange to this writer that the people who are presumed to have massacred them should subsequently commemorate them. That the folk of the Northern Isles are of significant Norwegian origin is well-attested both by the Orcadian place-names and by recent DNA testing. But the crucial question is whether these incoming men from Norway actually exterminated the local Picts, or the menfolk at least – the women are always presumed to have been left alive for obvious, if old-fashioned, reasons. It is hard, perhaps impossible, to prove a negative – but in this case, there is as yet no evidence for the "positive" idea of the massacre. Where did all the bodies go? Surely, we should have, somewhere, some mass graves?

Anna Ritchie's tidy Pictish houses appear to have early Viking dwellings built partially over them, but the latter seem to have contained only Pictish artefacts. A building that appears to be Norse adjoins the Pictish houses at Gurness, where a Viking woman with smart brooches was also buried. What are we to make of this? Anna was convinced that a peaceful coexistence was indicated, even if the status of those who had inhabited the Buckquoy houses was diminished. We will probably never know. There was always talk of warrior boat-loads arriving on the scene and going in for "ness-taking", occupying headlands of strength, perhaps like the Broughs of Deerness, Bigging and Birsay. Or it has been said that they threw up ramparts like those that may be seen beyond the Unstan cairn. Perhaps they occupied them, maybe even seasonally, for many years, and the two groups actually settled down to coexist. They must have done this in some places, such as the hinterland of Ross-shire, where Viking names like Dibidale and Amat (or in Assynt, Urigill and Traligill) testify to a Norse settlement within a Gaelic-speaking area. In such places, total domination by the incomers really seems impossible. In Orkney and Shetland, also apparently around Durness, things may have been different. Perhaps the Pictish men were either shipped off (where to?) as slaves, while others remained as serfs. The convenient, if gruesome, discovery of a few mass graves of slaughtered Pictish men would be a great help here. All we can reasonably say is that at some time, certainly by 800 AD, but possibly significantly earlier, the Vikings had arrived, and the Picts disappeared from sight.

Twelve

Around the Broughs

I am the sort of person who has a few favourite birds: the osprey, perhaps from the excited days of my youth; the Manx shearwater, from wonderful trips to the Small Isles; and the lapwing, that almost heraldic bird, which I associate so much with Orkney. And flowers as well: the minute Scottish primrose, *Primula scotica*, which is found only in these islands and along the magnificent North Coast of Scotland, and the fabulous grass of Parnassus. The latter I have found in many special places, and it, too, does well in Orkney. Presumably in response to the bracing winds, it grows shorter and more sturdily here than I have seen it elsewhere, and there is often lots of it.

We used to pass a small patch on the walk from our house on the Links to the crest of Marwick Head, and at the right time of year, perhaps after the middle of July, it bloomed superbly around Yesnaby. Some years it would coincide with a good flowering of the deep crimson *scotica*, and the combination of the two, wonderfully intermixed, reminded me of a renaissance tapestry; it was incredibly beautiful.

I found the *Parnassia*, too, right across Mainland Orkney, on the Deerness headland, on the North Sea coast. Here we would park close to the well-known Gloup, basically a very long sea-cave whose roof has partly fallen in. The splendid name can seem very onomatopoeic; with a wind from the east, the sea will rush in and slop around at the end of the open cave, the sound being magnified by the rock formation. Once, fairly carefully, I went there in a thick fog, and the sound of the sea combined fantastically with the eerie whistle of another favourite bird, the smart black guillemot or tystie.

At the seaward end of the cave, where there is a narrow geo, if you stand on one side you can get very good views of yet another special bird, the fulmar. Here they sit around at the top of the low cliff, almost at eye level. They lay just one egg, which they park, as it were, on a ledge, and this gives you a splendid opportunity to observe the young birds as they develop; initially, they look rather like a child's toy, a ball of down or fluff featuring a prominent bill and two dark eyes. The fulmar was critical to the economy of the St Kildans, but it was not known in Orkney until comparatively recently.

Along the headland to the north of the Gloup the grass of Parnassus grows well, and the walk is pleasant, comparatively level and easy enough underfoot. On the right, the immense expanse of water is the North Sea, and you may look, if you wish, in vain for a glimpse of the distant Norwegian coast, marvelling perhaps at the hardihood of the Vikings, who crossed these great open expanses. It may look calm, burnished silver some days, but on others it is wild and frightening to the modern eye.

As we continue northwards, across the rough grass, an obvious structure comes into view. It looks for a while as though we could simply walk to it. However, a short way on, some sort of bank or wall appears to stand between us and the ruin, although access still looks simple. A few more paces make it clear, though, that a vertical drop lies between us and the structure – a sudden drop to the sea. The bank or wall and the building visible behind it are situated on a dramatic, spacious rock stack, with cliffs virtually all round. There is a path snaking its cautious way up to the flat summit; reaching that path means tackling an awkward descent. This is a route that requires real caution when it is wet, and a good head for heights.

If you achieve both the descent and ascent, you will find yourself behind what is possibly a rampart, on the flat summit of a naturally defended headland, with the remains of a short, rectangular, stone building and the grassy foundations of many longer structures. In many ways, this, the Brough of Deerness, mirrors the Brough of Birsay on the western coast, but on a much smaller scale. It is a very strong position, defended by nature. The structures you see here are virtually all Norse, but there may be something older (in this case, possibly, the rampart that defends the weaker aspect), and there is a strong religious presence – the stone building here is a chapel. It has been suggested that both sites may have been monasteries (despite the lack of any written record), although much of what you see is actually domestic in origin.

But there are also differences: the most obvious being size. Deerness is an awkward, restricted site and, unlike Birsay, there is no room for grazing animals or growing crops. I have no faith in iso-lated communities without the necessary infrastructure for life, and doubt that the quite sizeable community inferred from the number of buildings here could have survived solely by fishing from the rocks or eating the local puffins (surely everyone's favourite bird, nowadays). If I were a local enthusiast I would be looking hard for a neighbouring farm or fields across the vertiginous gap. However, the vegetation looks rather unpromising apart from the obvious, much-improved new fields, and I have never seen anything relevant on my admittedly brief visits. The Mull Head, just a little bit further on (possibly a Celtic place-name, meaning bald or bare), is now mar-itime heath, with much crowberry and luxuriant tormentil. Does this awkward site make sense as a strong location, occupied early on by the incoming Vikings? Did their occupation thereafter perhaps result from the prestige of the strong place, until most of them left to live in greater comfort on the adjacent Mainland of Deerness? If so, there are real parallels with what we know of Birsay.

In this much more spacious location, it makes a lot of sense to walk around the perimeter of this attractive tidal island. I tend, therefore, to avoid the guardianship site at the beginning and head south, along the level ground above the low cliffs. There is a fine view of the cliffs of Marwick ahead, and, increasingly, the panorama of the bay, with its rock-ridges where the seals haul out, backed by the cluster of houses around the conspicuous ruins of the Earl's Palace. When you reach a fine geo, which almost cuts off the feature known, inevitably, as the "Peedie Brough", you start to ascend, and as you gain height, the views simply get better and better. (I used to drop down here, to another safe location from where it was possible to look along the seabird ledges, but there is now no point as they are empty.) As you reach the highest section, approaching the lighthouse, you get some sense of the importance of this island. The tidal channel provided the inhabitants with a moat that was regularly filled, and virtually all the perimeter is defended by cliffs, some high and overhanging. From the higher points, the view is magnificent, and on a good day extends southwards towards and along the coast to Cape Wrath, the "turning-point" of the Norse. To the north, you see the low snout of Rousay and the Noup Head cliffs of Westray, and much of the ocean in between. It would be very hard for a single ship, let alone a fleet, to approach unseen, and the vista includes the bays on either side of the causeway where such boats might anchor. (There was presumably some kind of portage place here, an easy way to pull longships over the very narrow strip between the bays, so that if the wind was too great from one direction, it was easy enough to launch from the other, sheltered bay.) The landward view is extensive, too; you can see a reasonable distance north and south, and further into the West Mainland, certainly to the end of the loch of Boardhouse, in the direction of Dounby. Admittedly, the effectiveness of this field of vision depends somewhat on the nature of the vegetation at this period of history, but much of the neighbourhood must have been farmed, and I think no one postulates any remaining woods in such an exposed location. So these critical sight-lines would actually have worked. A large body of men, mounted or otherwise, would have been seen from a significant distance.

(There are other things to look out for while on this circuit of the Brough. We once looked down and saw three porpoises, of different sizes, quietly nosing around the rocks. They appeared regularly, if briefly, on the surface, their small fins rotating as if on an invisible wheel. To speculate was inevitable: daddy, mummy and baby? A far less cosy view, in every way, came on a cold, grey day: half a dozen high, almost vertical fins, moving fast, close together, heading north. Killer whales on the move, they were menacing even to us on the cliff-top.)

To continue on the circuit of the island, doubling back along the fence around the site gives a good perspective of the excavated monuments, and takes you past the water supply that must have sustained the population. A number of small springs break out at this level, a reminder of the practical limitations imposed by the site, however attractive its defensive qualities must have been to the first settlers. As you follow the fence down to a small gate, close to the edge of the grass, it is worth halting here to consider the very name of the place you are visiting.

This is Birsay, "Byrgisey", the "built-up" or "walled" island. The first part of the name relates to "burg" and "borg", words for strong places; the second element is, of course, the word for an island, appearing all over the archipelago. There is a suggestion of strength, and we have seen how well fortified the site is by nature. As we at first walked along the low, level cliff, there was a wall on the left, above the crags, facing the sea. Against it, in places, were structures of some kind, huts or workshops perhaps. The crucial thing is that they were behind a wall, which was probably continuous and extended as far as the Peedie Brough where the higher cliffs begin. This is a very defendable place.

A site tour would begin with a consideration of the symbol stone of the Picts, and the possible early graveyard and chapel, to which I have already referred. Then, moving southwards, towards the end of the enclosed area, you can see long buildings with rounded ends running up the slope. Their thick walls are of turf, faced with stone, which should have kept draughts out. But there are several doors, which surely did the opposite? You may also see the low platform on either side of the paved area up the centre of the aptly named longhouse. Another structure has a drain running out from the lower end; cattle were probably stalled here. These buildings are interpreted as farmhouses and related structures of the early Norse settlers (the features I have mentioned used to be very clear in the days when everything was tidily strimmed by Historic Scotland, but recently an area has been left to grow, for the benefit of the wildflowers and nesting birds, obscuring much of the detail of the buildings). It is probable that the first part of the island, beyond the modern fence, was where crops were grown, and beyond that, the sweet grass was grazed. From the village, in the low, angled sun of bright winter days, a ditch and bank come down the slope of this open area, presumably the division between the two zones. (If you keep a look out, as you walk towards the Peedie Brough, this important feature is still visible.)

In strict chronological order: bypass the church and head for the structures below it, between the graveyard wall and the (concrete) cliff edge. Ignore for the time being the huddle of small rooms at the upper level, which I imagine derive from the period after power and the powerful had drifted away from the site. Under them are, I think, the remains of four or five large Viking houses, perhaps larger than the farmhouses on the slope; dare one think of them as halls? These are in a close group, and access to them from the original shore is provided by two roads, both paved, one with a covered, central drain. (Again, the original description of these as nousts ignores practicalities, and tends, perhaps understandably, to reduce one's faith in Ralegh Radford's commentary.) On either side of the road whose paving remains clear, smaller structures appear to have been inserted into older ones. One has been interpreted as a sauna (and seems to show many signs of heating), while the other appears to have a raised floor (Historic Environment Scotland believes this also to be a sauna). There is, visibly, a system of drains running through this part of the complex, but how it actually worked is quite beyond my comprehension, despite countless puzzled visits. We can also, of course, have no idea of how much of this section has been lost to the sea.

The real significance of this last paragraph is up to the reader. Does this complex of four or five large buildings (of the old style), accessed by two good roads, well-drained, with later, rather luxurious additions, simply amount to just more farmhouses, or would we be justified in thinking of it as "high status"? It seems to me that there is no credible alternative to the latter view. If anyone is worried about a lack of "ordinary houses", the space between the guardianship site boundary fence (behind the little museum that is now nearly always shut), and the edge was being excavated when I was living there, and was packed with structures of the appropriate period (another good place for a site marker!). The whole area is always described as a settlement, but given that we know that urban centres of this period were actually quite small, and that we have no idea how much we may have lost, it has long seemed to me that "small Norse town" might be a more appropriate description.

We do not have to follow Radford in naming one of these big buildings "Earl Sigurd's Hall". But given the secure nature of the site, its likely high status during the Pictish period, and this comparatively formal arrangement of large buildings, it seems somewhat perverse to deny the possibility, even probability, that the later Earl Thorfinn, at least, was based here. It is, of course, always possible that under Robert Stewart's Palace (of which more later), there may lurk the remains of the palace of the St Clair Earls (to which Raymond Lamb refers), and under that, an alternative for the site of Thorfinn's residence. However, at the moment, we do have a high-status cluster of structures on the Brough, and we have to come to some view on it.

This point becomes critical in assessing the remains of the (mercifully undoubted) church above the halls. (That it is there is possibly the only thing on which there is agreement.) The ruins themselves do not give much away, and the worry persists that there may have been rather a lot of tidying up after the excavations. The fact that the plan is – almost – standard for twelfth-century small (often parish) churches elsewhere may possibly be misleading. The intention was presumably to have a west tower or porch above the entrance into the nave. Beyond that, there is a chancel and apse – all of which seems appropriate, I agree, for the twelfth century. What is different is the presence of two semi-circular recesses on either side of the chancel arch (presumably for altars), which are unlike anything I have ever seen. Radford confidently identified them as later insertions, as he also did with the door into the enclosed court, and subsequent writers seem to have been happy to follow him. I confess that I would like a little more evidence (and remain surprised that neither he, nor, as far as I know, anyone else has had anything to say about the strange break in the stonework of the apse).

It so happens that during my time in Birsay we enjoyed a week's visit by members of the Cumberland and Westmorland Antiquarian and Archaeological Society. This was at that time considered to be a highly reputable group, and its members included some very knowledgeable and well-travelled figures. We spent a long time (another gorgeous day!) on the Brough, quite a lot of it in the church, and a number of them decided that its layout was that of a small, simplified, roman basilica. In particular, they referred to the altar-recesses on either side of the chancel arch, a comparison that, it has to be said, makes quite a lot of sense. This idea, of course, also made sense in light of the story that Thorfinn built a fine church on his return from Rome, possibly around 1050 AD.

This church subsequently became the first cathedral in the archipelago, the first fixed seat of a bishop – who may well, of course, have lived in the rooms across the sheltered court, as Radford postulated. What could be more natural than Thorfinn building this new church on the site of an older one, certainly within a sacred area, and close to his own residence? There he could (later) keep the activities of the new bishop under his watchful eye, while enjoying the continuing prestige of his foundation.

It is worth adding two brief comments. First, if the church on the Brough is twelfth century, as has been suggested, some pieces of (genuinely) red sandstone might have been found, in emulation of St Magnus' Cathedral in Kirkwall. Such stonework was found both in Eynhallow and Rousay, and appeared also in the structure that underlies the Church of St Magnus in Birsay (claimed from time to time as Thorfinn's Cathedral). Secondly, it is sometimes said that the building on the Brough is too small for the alleged purpose, but if we are discussing a cathedral church of the eleventh century (rather than twelfth), it seems to me we have few models with which to compare it. When I was young, many books used to point to the small size of the church founded in Dunfermline by Queen Margaret of Scotland, probably around 1070, a comparison that might still be valid.

The supply of water from the springs is, of course, important, whether you are enjoying saunas or not, and I presume it would have reduced as the climate improved throughout the twelfth and thirteenth centuries. This would perhaps have added to the pressure to move to the adjacent corner of Mainland Orkney, or to the growing urban centre of Kirkwall.

Thirteen

Changing Ideas

In a very short period of time, between perhaps 800 AD (by which time the effective occupation of the Northern Isles by the Vikings must have been well underway) and 1137 AD (when work began on the cathedral of St Magnus in Kirkwall), the leaders of the people achieved a remarkable transformation in image. At first, they tended to be regarded only as heading warrior bands, despoilers of monasteries, rapists, pillagers and pagans. By 1137, however, they had become cultured, Christian and, obviously, "well-travelled". One of their number, Thorfinn "the Mighty", whom we have already met, had made the considerable journey first to Hordaland in Norway, then to Aalborg in Denmark, through Germany and ultimately to Rome. In Scandinavia he stayed with the kings, in Germany he met Emperor Henry III, and in Rome he had an audience with Pope Leo IX, who granted him absolution for his sins (of which there must have been a few). This is impressive progress.

By this stage, the leaders had also acquired a title, that of "jarl". Although this is normally translated as "earl", it is actually quite far removed from the comparatively modest status implied by that title. I have always translated jarl as "semi-independent prince" but that would really require quite lengthy qualification. Effectively, one might say, the jarl headed an area almost like a principality, but one that owed allegiance to Norway – and which sometimes needed to be reminded of that fact. This is a subject, and a period, of great complexity, when Shetland, Orkney and Caithness were linked in what historian Dr Barbara Crawford has described as "a tripartite maritime lordship". Sometimes there were two earls within Orkney, sometimes the Earl of Orkney was also the Earl of Caithness. For further elucidation, the interested reader must consult Barbara's magisterial work, *The Northern Earldoms – Orkney and Caithness from AD 870 to 1470*. (I first met Barbara when her husband, Robert, brought some of his botany students from St Andrews to our little field centre, which became an annual event to look forward to.)

To add to the complexity of this period, our understanding of it, at least in part, derives from the body of literature known as the Norse Sagas. Again, this is not simple. These are traditional tales, memories of past events and characters, perhaps, but also stylised, following particular traditions. They give us, for sure, the names of prominent individuals. Perhaps because this is the first time in the long history of Orkney that we actually have names, there has been a tendency, as the reader may already have noticed, to ascribe certain buildings to individuals named in the sagas. That tendency is, I guess, understandable, but should probably come with a clear "health warning". It certainly gives a lot of scope for debate!

Throughout this period, then, there was a lot of activity, and a lot of building, some of which we have already discussed. It produced what are thought to be some of the earliest stone castles in what is now called Scotland. Cubbie Roo's Castle on Wyre, with its central, small stone keep, must be one of these; it was much augmented at some later date. There is mention, too, of a "stronghold" on Damsay, and the "Castle Howe" in East Mainland may also be of this period. (Sadly, the last time I went there, the site was chaotic.) Rousay, the big island close to Wyre, contains a building called the "Wirk", whose fine stonework seems to form a stair-tower at the gable of a hall. I am not entirely sure that I understand this structure. The actual stair, which is visible, seems to work its way rather awkwardly from the hall, and although the lower storey of the tower certainly has thick walls, they are noticeably narrower at the first-floor level. But that does not really matter; what does is that this beautifully constructed building, which elsewhere would be regarded as a real treasure, is here neglected, with fine blocks of stone left to fall out of the walls. The chamber within the tower has nettles growing within it, and the immediate surroundings are normally left unstrimmed and over-grown. Looking on the internet, the Canmore site fails to record any official interest since 1982, and Historic Environment Scotland is otherwise silent apart from the scheduling of the site in 1993. It has been suggested that Walter Grant began his excavating career here. If so, it is hard to understand how or why the Wirk has been allowed to deteriorate in this way. Alas, it seems to be rather par for the course in Rousay, an island rich in archaeology, but which, since Grant's day, has seen important sites dug and then simply left to the elements and the cows. I think particularly of the Viking cemetery and the substantial noust at Westness, just a little way along the shore, neither of which is worth visiting (at least the Wirk has acquired an interpretative board).

This is a real disgrace; Rousay deserves much better.

This building itself stands beside a post-Reformation church, whose gables have been conspicuously buttressed. It is presumed to be on a much older site, perhaps that of a church contemporary with the tower, roughly similar to the pairing found on Wyre, and also on the Brough of Birsay. The latter, of course, does not have a castle, but there are other large houses with churches close by. Among the illustrations in Barbara Crawford's book on the earl-doms is a reconstructed scene "of the twelfth-century earldom seat of Orphir", which shows the round church of St Nicholas beyond the earl's timber longhall (another photograph shows what looks rather more like a stone undercroft for a later secular building). Of the old church itself, there remains only the apse, and because of the raised floor level (I do wonder why the floor of the nave was not established when the site was investigated), it is hard to appreciate this rather classical architectural morsel. Once, when I was young and agile, I leaped down to the floor of the apse, from which vantage point its dignity was restored; I have been very fond of it ever since.

In the days when churchyards were not kept ruthlessly tidy, clumps of star-of-Bethlehem made this one beautiful, and a fuchsia, normally heavy with exotic blossom, almost hid the headstone for Storer Clouston. He was one of Orkney's most important historians, a significant writer and excavator of a number of sites, although many of his conclusions have since been challenged. This graveyard also supplied me with a huge amount of my own family history. By the time I came to live in Orkney I knew a certain amount about the families from whom I am descended, including the fact that one of them came from this kindly district of Orphir, on the gentle shore of Scapa Flow. Close to the remains of the church is a red sandstone memorial, heavily carved, with much of the relevant family history inscribed on the back. I imagine that nowadays you could buy a decent car for the cost that this work would have entailed, and we were very grateful to the family who decided to pay for it!

When I last visited it, Tuquoy Church in Westray was being worked on by Historic Scotland, with lots of tape, black plastic and men with hard hats, which rather restricted our view of the building. This definitely belongs in the list of dignified smallish churches of the islands. These are virtually all built in the same, rather obvious way – as is almost every structure to which I have referred since the beginning of this book; the way that the sandstone itself is laid down. Because of the degree of conformity this imposes on the masonry of many structures, few details permit a confident dating on the conventional basis of architectural style. As a result, the design of windows and doors has generally been seized on and used to help provide dating information. But there are dangers in this approach. For instance, there may be several reasons why any one arch looks the way it does. A) Was it the latest fashion in architecture, so the mason, who had seen examples, did the best he could with the materials he had at his disposal? B) Had the local mason heard that arches were now being constructed in this shape and did he do his best to envisage and implement this? C) Had the mason simply worked out a way to bridge the gap with the materials he had? These distinctions may seem trivial, but they are one way of considering the church building on the Island of Eynhallow, which either had complex phases of building or an experimental local architect.

It rather resembles the church on the Brough of Birsay, in that it has a western porch (perhaps the base of a tower) attached to a rectangular nave and chancel. It has no apse, but the arches in the porch, into the nave and into the chancel, are, as I have hinted, all different in style, and could suggest regular alterations. As one, however, could be regarded as harking back to the Saxon, and another to the early Romanesque, I am inclined to leave this debate to others.

In this "run-up" to the great work in Kirkwall, there is one further, smaller church to be considered, one we have already visited in the quiet isle of Egilsay. This name, incidentally, instead of being derived from "Egil's Isle" – in other words incorporating a personal name – has been argued, with some authority, to have a Gaelic connection. It is thought to derive from the word now rendered in Scots Gaelic as "h-Eaghlaise", meaning, of course, a church. This raises all sorts of possibilities, as indeed does the building's great attribute: its one tall, striking round tower, which makes it stand out on the low island skyline. Its masonry, too, is different from other churches (although I have never seen it commented on – it might perhaps provide some clue as to the origins of the design). Does the possibly

Celtic origin of the name, allied to the shape of the tower, make an Irish connection more likely than that argued by Professor Eric Fernie – that it derives from East Anglia and elsewhere around the southern North Sea?

It has been claimed that there were other churches in Orkney with round towers; two are generally mentioned in this context. One was at the location known as Skaill in Deerness (passed on the road to the Gloup and the Brough of Deerness), and drawings of it were made by the Reverend George Low in 1774. While the towers might possibly be Romanesque, they are either significantly shorter than that of Egilsay or the church building is much taller. (Some commentators suggest that the towers were at the east end, facing out to sea, but I clearly see a doorway there, in the centre of the gable, which makes this most unlikely.) The other was the Old Church in Stenness, where excavations apparently revealed that there had been a semi-circular tower, sitting on rectangular foundations. I am not sure how this works! It may be best, certainly simplest, to leave the church of St Magnus, Egilsay, as a spectacular piece of architecture, belonging somewhere in the twelfth century, earlier rather than later as far as I am concerned. It is very well preserved; in fact, it could easily be roofed. But one more question remains: how on earth was it lit? The walls are almost without windows, and the chancel, with its barrel vault, is very dark even now. Notwithstanding the strength of this remarkable building, the contrast with what was next to be built, in Kirkwall, is enormous.

The cathedral still dominates the old grey town of Kirkwall. Although its exterior is very interesting from the point of view of the architectural historian, it does not work so well aesthetically, and the visitor is advised to go straight in, through the remarkably heavy doors. First-time visitors should walk slowly down the middle of the nave, between the imposing pillars of the arcade, while their eyes accustom themselves to the generally rather low light. The first stop is at the crossing, where you are effectively surrounded by the oldest parts of the building. The actual crossing itself must have been rebuilt at quite an early point, so the first church is best seen in the three bays of the original short choir, and in the transepts, as well as the closest, lower part of the nave up which you have just walked. It is often said that "Norman towers fell like ninepins", so it is possible that the early rebuilding here was on structural, rather than stylistic grounds. For much of its history, the building must have had temporary walls and roofs, as well as the mediaeval equivalent of scaffolding, and, in general, there must have been a lot of noise and dust.

I tend at this juncture to walk into the choir, to look at the interesting range of carvings in the stone, and at the pillars where the bones of the founder and the patron saint of the cathedral are still. This is the part of the building I love best, and I normally cannot resist pointing out which was my stall; I was at one stage asked to sing with the cathedral choir, among whom I had many friends, and memories of that time are very special.

An important stylistic decision was taken when the original east end (which was presumably an apse on a grand scale) was removed and the church significantly extended. Although they look very thirteenth century in detail, the round arches hark back to the Romanesque style of the rest – one of the critical factors that lends a real feeling of unity within the building, despite the presence of the wooden organ case. This newer east end, now the St Rognvald Chapel, houses a number of memorials. Some are modest plaques on the wall, such as those to George Mackay Brown, his mentor Edwin Muir and other literary and historical figures. Others are rather larger; one with a recumbent statue is to John Rae, whose reputation as an Arctic explorer has in recent years been firmly re-established. He was a very pragmatic Orcadian, who, when faced with the challenge of surviving in the Arctic, adopted the mode of travel and clothing of the people who had survived there for centuries, if not thousands of years. (My grandmother believed we were related to him, and had one or two stories that seemed to confirm the idea, but I have so far not been able to prove this.)

Passing the memorial to the men of HMS *Royal Oak* (to which I shall return), with its ship's bell and the book containing the names of all 833 men who died, a Romanesque wall arcade leads down the length of the twelfth-century church. I have little intention of venturing much further into the architecture of this wonderful building. There exists an important book, *St Magnus Cathedral and Orkney's Twelfth Century Renaissance*, edited (this time) by Barbara Crawford. In it, there are chapters specifically on the building by Stewart Cruden, Richard Fawcett and Ronald Cant (a splendid cast!), which the interested reader is advised to consult.

There are, however, two points that I feel worth mentioning here. One is the matter of proportions; it has often been pointed out that for a church of the first rank, St Magnus is very short, at about 200 feet in length. This compares, for instance, with Southwell Minster at about 300 feet, and Ripon Cathedral at slightly less – and both are very much among the smaller of the English cathedrals. And although it is generally agreed to derive from the incomparable architecture of Durham (via Dunfermline), it is markedly smaller. It shares, however, with Dunfermline (the Romanesque nave of which is still impressive despite the travesty of the flat roof with which it has been saddled for decades) a feeling of height and narrowness that completely distinguishes it. The nave of Southwell, for instance, despite its many attractive details, is earthbound where St Magnus soars. When both the nave and choir were shorter than they now appear, the effect must have been remarkable, just possibly reminiscent of Norwegian stave-churches.

The other, critical aspect is the choice of stone for the interior. Much of it is red, its gentle warmth giving the building a truly special quality. Its architecture is splendid, anyway, but the overall effect would have been very different had the stone been a hard grey. This effect would have been denied to users of the building through much of its early years, however – we can clearly see that some of it, at least, was plastered and painted, including the massive piers of the arcade. In places, some yellow sandstone alternates with the red, which almost gives it a French or Mediterranean feel. I heard whispers once of a tradition of Italian masons working in southern Germany before going on to Norway and, possibly, thence to Orkney.

In a sense, little of this matters. St Magnus is an astonishing achievement and a truly beautiful building. This, and all that went with it, represents Orkney at its zenith. Despite the fact that I am no longer a church-goer, nor even a believer, it is a building I love. There was one day, all those years ago, when, although I knew it well by then, it managed to appear quite different from usual. It was the first of a few days of really sudden heat (there were four of these extraordinary days and then, as can happen in the islands, the fog rolled in – and stayed in). But this first day was amazing, a revelation, and I was in town. Every window and door that could be opened was open, and everyone who could be was outside. Every seat or bench or window-ledge was occupied; girls suddenly produced brilliant summer frocks, boys wore unaccustomed shorts and vivid T-shirts. Everyone was chatting, laughing, flirting, smiling; it was like a Mediterranean town (albeit one whose inhabitants had pale skins). The cathedral doors – all its doors – were flung wide open. Light flooded through them in brilliant blocks and, because the building was being used that evening for some theatrical event, all of the chairs had been removed from the nave, allowing me to see the true proportions of the building, the huge, rose-red pillars heaving upwards into the violet and blue shadows. Folk wandered in off the Street, young and old, local and visitor, and then the organist started to play. The old building was alive, and at the heart of the community of the isles.

Fourteen

The Rolling Year

Days of real heat, like those I mentioned at the end of the last chapter, were unusual, but on looking back at the journal I kept during the Orkney years, I am surprised at how much warm weather we actually had. In the course of a season, which might well be twenty weeks long, when I was out in the countryside six days a week, we always had some lovely weather; never a terrible summer like that of 2015. I lost very few complete days because the weather was truly foul – perhaps one per season. Even the lover of Orkney has to admit that Orcadian weather can be grim. There are days when the lack of shelter means that even the hardiest individual agrees heading for home is the best option. It was generally breezy, frequently windy, but often enough, if the morning was showery, the afternoon would be dry and bright – or vice-versa – and the day could work out quite well. Having said that, in those long-ago days, when there were far fewer visitors to sites such as Maeshowe or Skara Brae, and fewer folk on the ferries to Rousay or Hoy, I had more flexibility in planning my daily programme. Sometimes, we just had to go out and see what would happen. Worst of all were the extraordinary conditions accurately described as "seventy-mile-an-hour fog"!

Autumn, or a taste of it, might come early. Only a few days after such wonderful heat, there might be a real gale in August, and all the vegetation by our walks would suddenly be brown and tattered, especially near the West Coast. Sometimes we took our guests to one of the agricultural shows. I always cherished the idea of wandering around the Dounby Showground on an idyllic summer day, meeting and chatting to friends, admiring the beautiful, placid animals. The reality, however, was occasionally very different, with tents and stalls flapping madly or blowing away completely, squally showers blasting across the open field and the (very few) guests who had brought umbrellas rapidly looking at the wreckage the wind made of them.

The weather might recover from this blasting, but the wildflowers never really did, and crops could be irretrievably flattened. In those days, quite a lot of barley was grown. I remember one year when the large corner field by the loch of Boardhouse, which I passed almost every day, was sown with barley and ripened triumphantly, deepening to a glorious colour. In such wonderful conditions, the inland parish of Harray, with all its lovely farms, could genuinely glow like gold, backed by the blue-brown of the hills. Having few trees, and those being mostly sycamore, which don't "do" autumn colours, September and October were much subtler months than you see further south, just as I experienced on my return to Orkney in October 2015.

For us, Hoy, especially the North End and Rackwick, had the same relationship to the rest of Orkney as the Highlands do to the rest of Scotland: it was somewhere wild, relatively unpopulated and free. (We once had a wonderful short winter trip with dear friends from Kirkwall; a jaunt to Rackwick and along the bay, when my then-youngest daughter, aged perhaps seven or eight, borrowed my stick and rucksack to be photographed as the intrepid explorer among the dunes at the back of the beach.) After the summer months of leading groups, being followed at every step by perhaps a dozen folk or more, I needed to escape, to run free. As the bookings declined once we were past the middle of September, I would take a few days off and head, on my own, for the wide spaces of Hoy. Here I would stay in one of the two hostels in the north, and rejoice in being disorganised, changing my mind continually about where I wanted to go, stripping briefly to swim in the bracing lochs, generally not behaving in the calm and efficient fashion that the working season demanded.

Late autumn and winter could be very windy; we might have one gale every year when the wind speed exceeded a hundred miles an hour. These were very dramatic occasions, especially when living in the exposed corner of Birsay. The bay is crossed by innumerable ridges of rock, easily seen at low tide. When the wind is blowing, these cause the ocean to back up, to pile up until it looks like a tsunami wave about to sweep in and over the frail cluster of houses. Looking south, the cliffs rise up towards the crest of Marwick Head, which is almost 300 feet (we never thought in metres then) above the sea, which would now appear to be running halfway up it, a stream of spume pouring inland over the low houses. In the other direction, we looked towards the Brough of Birsay. I recall that when this huge wind was from the northwest, the spray towered twice the height of the lighthouse, and rivers of water poured down the eastern slope, which in the spring would be tranquil and covered with flowers. The noise was considerable: the wind howling, screaming through fence and telegraph wires, the waves crashing on the shore, and every now and then a muffled explosive sound, the effect of air in the sea-caves being fiercely compressed and suddenly released. This sent palpable shocks through the rock strata, which we could feel some hundreds of yards back from the turmoil.

If the gales were extraordinary, their after-effects could be just as remarkable. Apart from spending time outside the house, anxiously checking that no part of it had been blown away, or gloomily surveying the damage done to the garden, it was always worth going down to the shore for some beach-combing. There might, for instance, be some good fish-boxes; joy when we found a good, whole one, preferably wooden and marked "return to Lochinver"! Sometimes the beach looked extraordinary. On one occasion it was covered by the corpses of hundreds of baby octopuses, like pink, rubber bath toys. Another time, lots of the big seaweed, the kelp, had come ashore, but it had lost all its fronds and the root-like attachments that anchor the thick stalks to the seabed. These had a particular resemblance, and I was amused, some time later, to be at an exhibition in the Pier Arts Centre, Stromness, of works by a young, experimental, and forthright artist, who blithely referred, entirely accurately, to "phallus-strewn shores".

Because we were so low-lying – surrounded by water and washed in salt – frost and snow were rare. Sometimes our weather conditions were totally unlike those further south. My mother had the habit, out-of-season, of phoning us at ten on a Sunday morning (as mothers do), and one day the temperature in Birsay, on a February morning, was twenty-six degrees Centigrade higher than it was in Cupar, Fife. She was looking out at a snow-covered, totally frozen garden, most of the windows masked by frost-flowers (anyone remember them?), while I looked across the green Links to a smooth, silken sea under an azure sky. We did occasionally have snow; it so happened that the day after we moved into our house, we woke to a few inches of perfect snow, coupled with brilliant sun. A couple of days later, after some chaotic and exhausting unpacking, we decided to go for a short walk in our new surroundings. I well remember the beauty of that day, the smooth shapes of the snow-blanketed land, the sweep of the beach and the headlands, the strength of the farms on the skylines, the huge sky overhead – and that fact that when we met groups of others out for a walk (it was a Sunday), they stopped and spoke to us. Coming from Assynt, which in those days was strongly Sabbatarian, it felt like another world.

Under such rare conditions we looked out for the Northern Lights, and were once rewarded by a display of extraordinary beauty. I had nipped out for a look before bedtime, and realising what was happening, went in, told my wife, and we woke the girls and made them wrap up well before coming out into the brilliant night. We walked out onto the grass in front of the house, crisp with frosted snow, from where we could see all around – but it was upward we needed to look. It was as though we were in a huge tent, but the sides of the tent, which soared to the zenith, were neon panels of soft pink and an acid green, which flashed on and off above our heads. We stood transfixed, losing all sense of time – the heavens were ablaze with an unreal beauty, the like of which I have never seen since.

The winter was surprisingly good for watching hen harriers from the house, especially from my funny little office over the front door, which had a neat little gazebo (where mostly I grew pot plants, *Primula scotica* from seed, and could work when it was sunny). The harriers were attracted to our garden, largely and indirectly because of the habits of our cats, which enjoyed supplementing their rations with raids on the large rabbit population. They were very skilful hunters (unlike our dog, which was always distracted by the sheer number of potential targets) and very thorough in their consumption of the quarry – the only residue left normally seemed to be some pieces of fur, which blew around the garden and must have looked like somewhat vulnerable voles to the passing harriers.

Winter was, of course, the season when we had time for a lively social life (enormous fun), community activities of one sort or another (ditto) and the girls' regular ballet classes – which could be fun, too. The rehearsals and performances tended perhaps to be somewhat more fraught, but again, there was a strong sense of community among the attendant parents, and the occasional moment of beauty and emotion when watching the actual shows. Both girls were very graceful dancers, and really seemed to enjoy what they were doing.

February, in those days, still often brought a spell of beautiful, dry, mild weather, but it was beginning to shorten and be more erratic. The days were spent establishing a garden in the extremely sandy soil around the house, and the evenings in making my way to Kirkwall, for the rehearsals and then the performances of the Kirkwall Amateur Operatic Society, in whose productions I had for a while one or two leading roles. The best ever was in fact my first: as the Wandering Minstrel in *The Mikado*, which rather tested my limited musical ability but suited my voice. Much more significantly, it gave me an enormous amount of fun with a splendid group of folk.

March could be wild, cold and variable, and still there seemed to be no movement at all in the vegetation, nothing growing anywhere except in the very sheltered little "formal garden" that hid among the exuberant bushes of the wonderful *Rosa rugosa*. This thrived in the sandy soil and ignored the salty winds. But at some stage, a fashion for planting long lines of daffodils beside the roads (main, side and farm-tracks) had really taken off in Orkney, and the spring country-side was made lovely. Next came the dandelions in the fields, which were very clearly free from chemical weedkillers. Many of the fields were transformed into heavenly blocks of yellow, although not as acid as the colour of oilseed rape, which in later years a few farmers attempted to grow. By then, spring was well established, and we often had a longish spell of wonderful weather, with the wild ocean of the winter now calm and peaceful, lapping gently at the edge of the long beach. The seals basked on the rock ridges in the bay, their singing audible from the garden where we were planting vegetables and revelling in the soft air. By then the shelduck had taken over their burrows in the rabbit warren, and were enjoying their short court-ship flights, often across the green road that led past our house and across the Links. I can still hear their soft cackle. There were perhaps two dozen birds, so it was a lively scene. The adults must have been fairly effective in seeing off the cats, as I never had to tidy up bits of duckling; it may be the cats had turned their attention to the rats, which in any farming community can be rather numerous.

But the great sign of the changing year was the return of the seabirds, especially, in those years, the great numbers of kittiwakes on the cliffs. These gathered in large flocks, perhaps a thousand birds at a time, settling for a while on the exposed ridges of rock in the bay, before suddenly erupting like whirling snowflakes and heading over our house to the loch to splash and bathe. They called continuously as they flew, and provided some wonderful moments.

Throughout the year, we often found ourselves in the two very different towns of Kirkwall and Stromness. Since I had started taking visitors to see them, I had begun, probably for the first time ever, to enjoy urban spaces. I had always loved Edinburgh, the great city of my youth, where visits were very special and fairly rare, but Edinburgh is beautiful by any standard, and I had had no interest in most ordinary towns. Admittedly, in foul weather, both Kirkwall and Stromness can look fairly grim. Fortunately, we soon established in each that perhaps most precious category of friend: the family you can drop in on while on a shopping trip or whatever, and be offered, immediately, a reviving cup of coffee – and perhaps a gossip as well.

The sandstone of both towns looks warm and attractive in the sun. Both have narrow vennels to explore, especially Stromness, where some lead down to old piers and the sea, and others up the hill. Both towns, too, have gardens, bushes and trees. The latter are generally sycamore, of course, and some are home to the rooks that go out into the fields – noisy and messy birds as far as some are concerned, but again for me an important part of the past. In this case, it was our old stone house in Cupar; from our bedrooms we looked out towards the Lomond Hills that back the fertile fields of the Howe of Fife (nothing to do with Norse mounds in this case!) and in the evenings, against the distinctive silhouette of the hills and the sunset, the long, noisy lines of rooks flew overhead. Some nested in the yews on either side of our drive.

Fifteen

Palaces

In the years running up to 1137, Kirkwall must have been a very small community, located on its convenient isthmus, with its sheltered harbour (now the very shallow inlet known as the Peedie Sea) and its church. After 1137, it saw an enormous effort of construction, a noisy labour that went on for decades, indeed into the following centuries. The building of the cathedral was, of course, the great work. The rearing-up of a building of unparalleled size for the islands, a construction that must have been, literally, awesome to the folk of the settlement and those from the surrounding countryside. But it was not alone; far from it. The Bishop, after all, was coming to town, in order to live beside this house being built for God, in which he would, as soon as physically possible, start to hold services. So he needed a palace, and work began on that around the same time. You may still see the ghost of yellow and red sandstone detail around the windows of the lower level of the now-ruined building that was modified, rebuilt or stabilised through the following centuries.

It is also possible that he built a summer palace, somewhere to visit in the warmer months, close to the old site on the Brough of Birsay, but on the more accessible shore of the Mainland. Here a new church was certainly being constructed around the same time – it lies under the Church of St Magnus, now situated in Birsay village.

And, of course, in order to be associated with this new centre of power both religious and economic, there came the Earl and his retinue, who also needed a palace in which to reside. Of this only the scantiest remains are to be seen – glimpses of the familiar red and yellow stonework below the level of the grille of the well on the ground floor of the later structure. It is enough to indicate that the Earl, too, made sure his presence was felt. All this work, the employment and the cultural activities that went with it, ensured that the quiet cluster of houses on the narrow isthmus was totally transformed after 1137, becoming one of the capitals of the far-flung Scandinavian world.

Taken with the previous waves of building to which I have already referred – the churches, for instance in Orphir and Egilsay, and all the rest – this clearly represents a huge investment. Times were obviously good, and it will be no surprise that this all happened during a period of climatic optimum, when harvests must have been bountiful. Travel across the known world was easier than before, even to the once unknown world, to places such as Iceland, Greenland and Labrador. Orkney was a country of prosperity, known, cultured, its leader a figure on the European stage and even further afield.

Earl Rognvald, the founder of the cathedral and nephew of St Magnus himself, departed on a long expedition, part jaunt, part Crusade to the Holy Land, in 1151 AD. This underlined his status and, by chance, ultimately added to the cultural treasures of Orkney. Men who had been on this long voyage with him later took refuge, when back in Orkney, in the tomb of Maeshowe during violent weather. As is very well known, they left a remarkable collection of runic inscriptions. These are interesting from a scholarly point of view, as well as being rather beautiful to look at, but they are not exactly profound in content. I suspect that the various custodians who introduce the monument to groups of visitors are instructed to remain silent or vague about a few of the more basic, but the implication of some of these bits of graffiti is quite widely known.

An eminent scholar, emerging from the tomb, was overheard to remark: "It was quite clearly a Viking knocking-shop" (no, my lips are sealed!). Others have drawn similar conclusions. I do often wonder if I am the only person who would love some elucidation as to how this particular function of the Maeshowe chamber actually worked. How was the place made comfortable? Did someone look after it while it was unused? And were those who wished to take advantage of the facilities visible as they approached the great howe? All archaeological commentators seem sure that the tomb was prominent in a fairly empty landscape, one at best of fields, and certainly not dotted with woodland.

(Much of the information like this, about the surrounding environment, has come from the ditch around the monument. I used to show visitors the wonderful groups of orchids that grew there, but have seen on recent visits that sheep now graze around the monument, including in the ditch itself. Perhaps this has its convenient side as "bargain" grass-cutting at the site, but it has, unfortunately, destroyed the orchids.)

Work on the cathedral continued into the following centuries, but times were slowly changing. The background climatic conditions slowly deteriorated, which must gradually, once again, have made everyday life in these northern isles more difficult, just as it had after previous ages of plenty. The Black Death came in 1369, bringing its own dread and, of course, decimating the workforce available for any purpose. The rise to prominence and visible prosperity, evidenced during the twelfth-century building campaigns, probably attracted the attention, and greed, of both Norwegian and Scottish kings. This is a long and complicated story. The authoritative volume by Barbara Crawford has already been acknowledged; to it should be added the exhaustive *New History of Orkney* by William Thomson. Both are required reading for anyone who wishes to work their way through the complex details of the following periods, when the old line of earls was succeeded in turn by the Sinclair Earls and then the Stewarts. By this time Orkney had firmly become part of the adjacent country of Scotland.

It is known that the Sinclair Earls built a strong castle in Kirkwall, adding to the existing collection of remarkable buildings there. Nothing of it remains, apart, apparently, from its capped well, which is supposed to lie under Castle Street. In Kirkwall, a Scottish bishop, Robert Reid, propped up the hall of his collapsing old Palace, built the prominent round tower attached to it, and added to the length of the cathedral, incorporating the original west doors. The irony is that while he was stabilising his residence, the extension he added to the cathedral proved in the long run to be rather poorly built. When I came on my own in the late 60s, part of the stone vault was looking dangerous, and there was tape across the nave. (All that has, of course, long since been repaired, and the beautiful interior is as serene as ever.)

The incoming Stewart Earls – Robert, illegitimate half-brother of Mary, Queen of Scots, and his son Patrick – left a fairly grim reputation behind them, with which we are not concerned here, and some rather attractive architecture, with which we are. Robert must have occupied the old Palace in Kirkwall, but he built for himself a summer residence in Birsay. Its ruins dominate the little village and are in the keeping of Historic Environment Scotland, who refer to the building both as palace and castle. I suggest the use of the word "castle" is somewhat misleading. The cause may lie in the daunting array of gun-loops that greet the visitor, but these must have been mostly for show. When they were not actually in use (and there is little to show that they ever were), they would have to be blocked up, or the draughts would have made the building almost uninhabitable except in the rarest of conditions. And at the entrance (where the

Orkney flagstone, seen here along the Rousay shore, close to Midhowe.

The fertility of the soil derived from the sandstone is
shown in these wildflowers on Marwick Head.

The serenity of the Orcadian landscape in summer: Waulkmill Bay.

The tidal island of the Brough of Birsay, seen across the bay.

The High Island: Rackwick Bay in Hoy has its own special atmosphere.

The West Mainland in autumn, across Wide Firth.

Orkney wetland: The Loons, an important bird reserve.

The Victorian Orkney plantations are unexpected, luxuriant.

Orkney moorland: The open spaces of the Birsay Moors.

Orkney's second town, Stromness.

Jean Noble, nee Menzies,
Wren at Hatston in World War II.

Captain Donald John Munro, who
fortified Scapa Flow in World War 1.

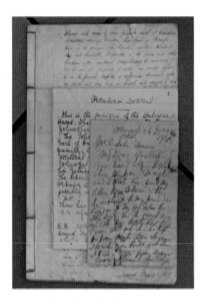

Orcadian family documents.

The *Meta* in Stromness harbour,
commanded by Capt. Thomas White.

Monuments in the landscape, Iron Age: The Broch of Gurness.

Monuments in the landscape: Farm buildings on Rousay.

Monuments in the landscape, Neolithic: The Ring of Brodgar.

A quiet autumn afternoon beside Scapa Flow.

little towers project at each end of the facade), although it looks as if no attacker could ever survive the fire from each side, in fact there would have been a real danger of badly damaging the opposing wall if the gunner ever missed a human target in the space between. Far more than this, however, Historic Environment Scotland don't mention the fact that the line of individual apartments on the western range of the courtyard had windows at the ground-floor level, facing the sea and the sunset. These are interesting rooms, not large, but each was provided with its own door, a fireplace and this western-facing window. The tall chimneys that adorn the west wing actually belong not to the Long Gallery, which was on the first floor, but to the rooms below, and this arrangement is, interestingly, paralleled at the romantic, rock-girt stronghold of Dunnottar.

At this juncture, it is worth saying that these blocked-up windows, which give entirely the wrong impression of the building, really should be revealed properly. In the time I have known it, Historic Scotland showed little understanding of this important building, which is, in fact, a fine, quadrangular manor. As I have said, part of it closely resembles a building within the complex of Dunnottar, the Palace Block, one wing of which, with a Long Gallery above, possesses a line of individual chambers, each with its own access and fireplace. This elegant block was built for the Keith Earls Marischal, "allegedly the richest nobles in Scotland". The authority on such buildings is Charles McKean, and the interested reader is urged to read his *The Scottish Chateau*, with reference both to Dunnottar and Birsay. The latter, lacking the naturally protected setting of the former, is in a more secure quadrangular form. The Palace at Dunnottar was probably built around 1580, and Charles McKean shows a conjectural reconstruction of the courtyard. Despite the comparative irregularity of this layout, the resemblance to Birsay, which is supposed to have been built between 1569 and 1574 (Historic Environment Scotland), is most marked. McKean shows a seventeenth-century drawing indicating that the corner towers probably had conical roofs, that there were no battlements, and that the north and east ranges, perhaps containing the earl's private apartments, had first-floor windows with very elaborate hood-moulds. The building had great lines of peat stacks (all those chimneys to keep burning!) on the west, but pleasant, enclosed yards on the east. Another, rather later, drawing shows the roof missing, but confirms the overall layout and elegance of the place.

(Most interestingly, it also shows the quite substantial remains of a church on the Brough, although it is declared to be ruined. Across the burn from the palace is a very substantial, three-storey, double-range building with a high wall around its own garden. This is declared to be the "Old Mance", but it is on such a scale that I wonder if this is not a more likely candidate for the missing Bishop's Palace than the burnside site that has been generally suggested, but on the vaguest of grounds.)

The type of facade built here at Birsay was very fashionable, even if, with its two storeys and three-floored towers at the corner, it was comparatively modest. The style – the contrast of high chimneys, probably with some decorative detail, the elaborate upper windows, (most probably also at Dunnottar) – reaches its apogee in the grandeur of Hamilton Palace, the home of another powerful and wealthy dynasty. Birsay, too, takes its place among significant buildings of Renaissance Scotland. The Historic Environment Scotland site quotes a description of its rooms from 1701: "prettily decored, the Ceiling being all painted ... with schemes holding forth Scripture – Histories, as Noah's Flood, Christ's riding to Jerusalem, etc."

Around the same time, another unsavoury Scot, Gilbert Balfour, was granted land in Westray, where he built himself a real castle. The original building, a Z-plan towerhouse, was never completed, but Noltland Castle still looks formidable. It has an incredible number of gun-loops, 71 in all according to Historic Environment Scotland. Again, it has to be doubted whether the castle would ever have contained enough men, let alone guns of one kind or another, to make proper use of this imposing array. Like Birsay, there are at least traces of refinement in the details of the upper-floor interiors. But it took subsequent occupiers to add a fine stairway, the courtyard and some ancillary structures, which must have made it more suitable for normal living.

It is probable that the elegant stair was added by Earl Robert's son, Patrick, who managed, possibly, to be even more hated than his father or Gilbert Balfour. He did a lot of building, including the fine tower of Scalloway Castle in Shetland. In addition, he probably altered his father's palace in Birsay, and transformed the old complex of buildings he inherited in Kirkwall. Most of what we can see of his new building uses fashionable, rather French, architectural detail, especially heavily corbelled oriel windows. An open-arched loggia joined the old Bishop's Palace to a range, now a private house that has been harled, obscuring any detail. But the intention was obviously to link this last structure to the gable of the building we know as the Palace of Earl Patrick (of 1601–07), at the heart of what was called the "Palace of the Yards". Charles McKean describes this as "a 'U-plan' villa... on a regal scale". Although it boasts the usual rows of gun-loops, with its enormous windows on the first floor, looking outwards as well as into the courtyard, it would have been impossible to defend from armed attack, let alone artillery. There is, however, a clear indication that Patrick was deeply concerned about his personal security; there was a shot-hole beside the main doorway and the "chambre a tirer" in the wall behind it is easily seen. I have never lain down there to see how well it functions if the intention was to gun down some undesirable individual approaching the main entrance. It is however very clear that if Earl Patrick felt he could trust a few men posted in the awkward little room under the stairs, he could rest easy in the spacious apartments upstairs, knowing that from there, they could keep under observation anyone who entered from the courtyard or via the "tradesman's entrance", as well as those in the kitchen itself. This is remarkable evidence of very careful planning, for which I know of no parallels, and backs up the description of Patrick, who "never went... abroad... without the convoy of fifty musketeers and other gentlemen of convoy and guard". It is perhaps not too fanciful to say that Patrick did fear assassination (quite a habit in the Renaissance?), and that the planning of his sumptuous palace reflects this.

It is not very easy to discern the fine details that distinguished Earl Patrick's building, as yellow sandstone erodes badly and much of the carving has weathered. The splendid windows facing outwards have totally disappeared. Worse, too, as far as I am concerned is, that during all the years of Historic Scotland's guardianship, little interest was shown in the structures themselves. In both palaces, doors and windows remained blocked or part-obstructed, and a few small, ugly, structural expedients were left in place for decades. The imposing stair up which Patrick must so often have trodden had soot on its walls; again, this has been there ever since I first visited. This is not the way to look after one "of the finest Renaissance Palaces in Scotland", as described in the invaluable RIAS illustrated architectural guide to Orkney. Historic Environment Scotland's website describes "a building of extraordinary refinement, spacious and masterfully planned". The treatment of it over the years was in sad contrast to the enormous exercise of scholarship, imagination and expenditure that, for instance, transformed the palatial structures within Stirling Castle. They have at least been fortunate, as so often in Orkney, in those who deal, on their behalf, with the public who come to visit these important places.

Sixteen

Carvings

The carved detail in the ruins of the Earl's Palace, mentioned at the end of the last chapter, is mostly heraldic. Some of it has gone; Earl Patrick's own arms were enthusiastically defaced at some stage, but the Royal Arms of Scotland, those of his grandfather, remain in place above the main door. That entrance itself has fluted columns on either side, perhaps topped by coronets, but the sandstone is so wasted that it is impossible to be sure. Inside, the same applies to the detail on either side of the huge fireplace in the Great Hall, but the ribs in the attractively vaulted little waiting room are reasonably clear. They must, of course, have been plastered and painted. There were texts, too, at the front entrance, but they, also, have largely gone.

This is, of course, the problem with much of the sandstone: it is soft and easy to carve, but this merely means that it erodes very easily in the harsh Orcadian conditions. The cathedral shows this all too clearly, and also highlights the great dilemma: what to do about, or with, the decayed stone. The doorway on the outside of the northern transept is a case in point. It uses the alternate colours of red and yellow most attractively, but some of the individual stones have been very badly weathered. These have been replaced, somewhat controversially, in that the new pieces stand proud of the older, and are extremely obvious. This has become something of a fashion in archaeological and architectural circles. Somehow, new replacement stones have to be glaringly evident, and it does not matter if this is to the detriment of the resulting aesthetic appearance. (Nobody seems to appreciate that if the date of replacement were to be carved quietly on one corner, it would be evident that this piece is not original.) Another example of this is the great west facade of the noble, but much-ruined Cathedral of Moray at Elgin, which has also had to suffer significant indignity at the top of the fine towers. At least there the replacement stone does not stand proud, and it will presumably darken through time, but at that door of St Magnus', the visual problem will remain, almost forever. The reaction to this work of restoration was, I well remember, almost unanimously negative, and so the notion of treating the very fine main west doors in the same manner was abandoned. There was then, I recall, a proposal to build a porch to protect the seriously decayed stonework; it was to be made of glass and steel, and that, too, met with a firm negative. Understandable as that reaction was, many years on, something still has to be done about the condition of the stonework here – time, once again, for some imaginative thinking? Could it, perhaps, be carefully cleaned (it still holds soot, too), then treated with some kind of matte, colourless resin to protect it from the elements? – just an idea.

Inside, there is a wonderful repertoire of carved detail, the latest of which are the amazing gravestones. Many date from the 1600s, a period of almost unbridled doom and gloom, replete with every symbol of mortality that the morbid imagination of man could devise. Judging by the carvings, the twelfth century also appears to have been full of horrors, imagined or real, and there are several strange heads, especially at the lower levels in the choir, half-human, half-animal or fish, eyes bulging and inimical. If you raise your eyes, preferably through binoculars, to the high stone vault and its corbels, the heads here, dating mostly from the thirteenth century, are comparatively normal and serene. Some of the carved bosses are of foliage, and one or two of the capitals in St Rognvald Chapel show little figures amid the leaves, with salamanders winding around the stonework. Sadly, the tracery of some of the bigger windows has inevitably suffered from centuries of rough weather, and has been largely renewed. Some of it seems to have been quite advanced in style – yet another indication of the fact that Orkney was really neither significantly behind-the-times nor backward in any sense.

The tendency to use ornamentation clearly goes back a long way. Apart from their runic inscriptions, which we have mentioned already, the band who broke into the tomb of Maeshowe that stormy day left a few tiny carvings. One of these, now known as the Maeshowe dragon, has become familiar to many through its use as a motif in the fine jewellery for which modern Orkney has rightly become renowned. Many such elements from the past, whether from carvings in the cathedral, or the runic writings themselves, appeared first in the inspired work of Ola Gorie, charming doyenne of Orkney jewellers. Where she led, many have followed: crafts-folk and artists from outside the islands, as well as the considerable talent available locally. As will, I hope, have become clear, colour is very important to me, and I particularly admire the work of jewellers who use enamel, so appropriate to the colouring of the shores and skies. Of these, Sheila Fleet has produced some superb designs. (This is a hugely talented family; visit her sister's Tapestry Gallery at Hoxa Head on South Ronaldsay, and you will see what I mean.)

There are enough carved Pictish stones in the archipelago to show that the islands shared in this period of creativity in stone. The stone from the Brough of Birsay was found in pieces, and a cast is positioned on site, but its detail is now almost invisible unless angled sunlight strikes across it (clearly time for a commissioned carved replica, please, Historic Environment Scotland?). Its symbols, when they can be seen, are both finely detailed and typical of the Pictish repertoire, with the famous, if vaguely named "Pictish beast", an eagle and a salmon and other, abstract shapes. The three process- ing figures in long robes, carrying tall spears and square shields, are unusual. Another, and rather different, but very fine eagle appears on a stone from the Knowe of Burrian in Harray, now in the Museum in Kirkwall. It also has an abstract symbol, the so-called "crescent and v-rod or broken arrow". Again, these would be fine motifs for jewellery, but I have not seen them so used. What the symbols actu- ally mean has been endlessly debated; there is perhaps a measure of agreement that they could "describe" an individual, a family or an extended group of people. They are clearly compatible with Christianity, as they are often found in a Christian context, or com- plete with a carved cross.

Back in the Neolithic, it appears that the desire to embellish, to beautify (or, perhaps, to convey something important, some sort of message or reminder), was as important as in any subsequent era. There are lots of carvings, mostly patterns made up of straight lines, which are easier, of course, to carve in stone. One motif occurs both on stone and in the pottery of the period: the chevron, which, so much later, reappears prominently in the Romanesque of St Magnus'. Other patterns include zigzags, lozenges, parallel lines and saltires. Many patterned stones have been found during excavations at Ness of Brodgar. There are also some at Skara Brae, a few of which are still in situ in the actual village; the edge of a bed in the now-in- visible house No. 7 is a good example.

Virtually all of the carvings of this time seem to be abstract, a repetition of straight lines that means nothing more to us now than decoration. Much, therefore, has been made of the tiny figurines that have been discovered, the first of which was dubbed "the Westray Wifie". Human representations from this era are extraordinarily rare in Britain, but we should not assume these rudimentary figures are anything more than toys, minute playthings for children. Had they wanted to, the Neolithic sculptors could no doubt have produced much better depictions of the human form. That they were capable of elaborate rounded forms is obvious. From Skara Brae, for instance, came a group of complex, carved stone balls, the creation of which must have demanded a considerable degree of skill. Supreme above all, so far, is the elaborate lintel from Westray, which was for a while in Tankerness House Museum, Kirkwall, before being returned to the island on which it was discovered (sadly, when I last saw it, it was sitting on the floor; I feel it should be raised up, highish, something to look up to and admire). It shows splendid, deep spirals and concentric circles. Inevitably, it is reminiscent of the great tomb of Newgrange in Ireland, suggesting that even so far back, Orkney was very firmly connected to the outside world.

I had previously suggested that the existence of the drainage scheme at Skara Brae was one of the true marvels of the New Stone Age, but something recently discovered at the Ness of Brodgar is at least as astonishing. In some of the structures in what has been described as a temple complex, some large stones in the walls of the interior spaces have been found to be painted – coloured with pigment. If anyone still clung to the idea that people this far back were "primitive" or "savages", surely these details must alter that view fundamentally. No doubt they were as capable of stupidity, cupidity and cruelty as our species has been ever since, but, like us, they had concepts of beauty or attractiveness, aspects on which they spent a considerable amount of time and effort.

For me, the greatest puzzle of all is why, during this period, there appears to be a strict prohibition against representation of the human form, or other aspects of nature, birds, flowers or animals, which surrounded them all the time and on which they depended for their lives. The discovery of the bones of animals and birds (dogs, otters and sea eagles, for instance) in some of the chambered tombs must indicate that there was at least some "official" acknowledgement of a relationship or connection between those creatures and the human population. Clearly, further discoveries may help us understand this particular puzzle. Until then, the simple fact remains that during the New Stone Age the Orcadians were as interested in the appearance of their buildings as they have been ever since.

Seventeen

After the Stewart Earls

Perhaps the best thing to be said about the period of the Stewart Earls is that it produced some fine buildings, however great a burden their construction was on the population. They, Robert and Patrick, were here in Orkney precisely because this was still almost "another country", somewhere remote from central authority (not remote enough, it turned out, for Patrick). But at least when he died, Patrick had left Kirkwall with buildings fit for a capital city, however little appreciated they might be. The following two centuries, moreover, were not good times. Slowly, the native character of the archipelago was undermined by incoming Scots and Scottishness. The old culture, customs and law came into conflict with the new, and generally lost out. There was almost constant feuding, it seems, at nearly every level of society – quarrels over land and religion, financial dealings of incredible complexity and general dubiety, all set against a background of repeated famine, poverty and death. There is plenty of factual evidence for all of this; for details see again William Thomson's *New History of Orkney*.

Despite this, the whole story is not necessarily one of doom and gloom. Some folk managed to do quite well, or managed to build themselves some fine houses, which we can see today. After the execution of Earl Patrick, his large landholdings were broken up, and Bishop George Graham acquired some land in the West Mainland. Here he built not one but two significant houses, both in fairly windy locations. Breckness House, dating from 1633, is well to the west of Stromness, with a fine view across to Hoy. It had two-storeys, on an "L" plan, with a simple but dignified, symmetrical facade, plus various outbuildings. Sadly, the building has been effectively abandoned to the elements; it at least ought to be consolidated and protected against further collapse.

His other house was on the Bay of Skaill, a fine courtyard mansion that dates from 1620, and forms the right hand, white-painted block as you look from Skara Brae. This house was much extended in later centuries, and is now Orkney's largest mansion. Fortunately, the extensions have all been done in a style sympathetic to the old part – moderately plain, with some gables crow-stepped.

Probably older is the Hall of Tankerness, on the eastern coast. This again is a plain house that was subsequently extended in complex ways. Additions included a conservatory, an "iron pavilion" and a low, round tower. It passed to the Baikie family – who also maintained a town house in Kirkwall, Tankerness House, which now houses the excellent museum – in 1630. It had begun as a subdeanery and archdeanery for the cathedral, but the whole complex was reworked in the eighteenth century. Not that far from the Hall, in Holm, stands a house I have long admired for the great visual strength of its front elevation. Greenwall was built by another Graham in 1656. In fact, Bishop Graham also had a property nearby, although it has since been much altered and is now called Graemeshall.

Most of the islands possess a house from this period. They are, in effect, precursors of what we normally call "Laird's Houses" in the Scottish Highlands. Most of the latter are of a later date, built some time during the comparative peace and prosperity that followed the chaos of the Jacobite Rising of 1745. Here in Orkney there are houses of this style and (roughly) date in Papa Westray (Holland House) and in Eday (Carrick House). Even little humped Gairsay has its fine house of Langskaill, which possesses the obviously very popular feature of a walled courtyard with arched entrance. There are a number more elsewhere.

At the same time as lairds and officials were building these, smaller but quite dignified stone houses were also being constructed, frequently, we must assume, by the wealthier farmers. Of them, Kirbuster Farmhouse is now maintained by the Orkney Museum Services. It bears a date of 1723, but either the stone was lifted from some other building or the date refers only to an altered part of the structure – or the house was built in an archaic fashion. Generally, it is assumed that it, too, is from around 1600; even in that context, it appears rather dated in some ways. It is the last of what are always called the "firehouses". What is remarkable about the fire in these is not the fact that there was one, but that it was freestanding, rather than within a gable. There is a small, low wall, in the main room, on one side of which the fire was kept burning. This was actually a very efficient arrangement, as it produced some sort of free-standing storage heater in the middle of the living space. There was a "lum" or hanging chimney, in the roof above, and an arrangement by which the draught could be regulated to suit the wind direction. Its other archaic features are the beds within the walls, an arrangement often said to look as old as Skara Brae, although, in fact, the beds there are in the main room, not inside the thick walls. But it is also quite dignified, with walls, (and, therefore, a roof) significantly loftier than most from that time – useful for those of us who are six feet tall. A number of other houses are thought to date from around this period, including Winksetter in Harray. Tofts in Quendale on Rousay, may be significantly older than that, but where documentation is lacking, it can be hard to decide from architectural details, which are often very few. The sandstone, too, imposes a logical way of building, adding a degree of uniformity.

But a discussion of Kirbuster requires some consideration of its cluster of surrounding buildings, and introduces yet another topic, or aspect of architecture, one where Orkney can again make great claims. This is the matter of what are called "vernacular buildings", the farm buildings and cottages with their ancillary buildings that began to appear, in general, in the 1600s and 1700s. The main characteristics of these Orcadian vernacular buildings are slab-roofs and, often, crow-stepped gables. The fishermen's huts at Marwick, roofed by large slabs, should be included in this category. Later structures, such as the byre at the Corrigal Farm Museum, show the enduring use of vertical slabs in much the same way as they were employed in the great tomb of Midhowe. These are very special buildings. The Click Mill we visited earlier in the book is one of a number that may date back to Norse times; it is one of the latest and best preserved. My favourite structures of all, I think, are the drying kilns. These were normally attached to a barn where the grain was stored. They are to be found all over. Rousay has several and there are two down by the Midhowe shore. Externally they may be squarish, or perfectly rounded, dumpy little towers, but inside they are beautiful. At the base, there is a carefully constructed bowl, into which a flue would bring peat smoke, which would then be drawn upwards through slats on which sat the grain to be dried (or given a good smoky flavour for brewing, perhaps even distilling). Above this, the stonework inches inwards, finely corbelled, like a miniature version of a tomb from Classical Greece, up to a hole in the roof, through which the peat smoke would exit. These are practical buildings, but they are also a truly lovely contribution to the architecture of the Northern Isles. I have never been sure why they are so scarce elsewhere.

I know that the importance of the vernacular buildings to Orkney has been officially recognised, for instance in council documents. There is, however, the problem of how to finance the preservation of so many such buildings. Context matters, of course. The Midhowe shore of Rousay has two small groups of buildings, one called Brough and the other Skaill, and both groups have kilns. One looks quite solid and sound, but at the other the peat-neuk built against and supporting the kiln-tower has disappeared and that part of the wall looks extremely precarious. This is at a most attractive point on the Rousay shore. It looks across the Sound, with its impressive tidal Roost, backed by big fields and dominated by high heather hills. These grey buildings, as so often in Orkney, fit beautifully into the landscape, but they are slowly collapsing, and one day will be featureless, to the detriment of the whole scene. You can read more about this vernacular architecture in another masterwork: *The Northern Isles* by Alexander Fenton.

Such ancillary buildings, whether for farming, fishing or storing produce, continued, of course, to be built into the eighteenth and nineteenth centuries, but they are mostly distinguished by their greater size, especially by their height. The use of native stone in the wall, local slabs in the roof, a few decorative features such as the crow-step gables all persisted, as seen in several cottages, too. Many have since collapsed, but some have been carefully restored and are delightful, inside and out; friends of ours, up over the hill into Marwick, had one, complete with box beds.

By now, I trust I have made it clear that Orkney's long history has produced an extraordinary architectural heritage, one that has to be of world stature. Indeed, by most criteria, the entire archipelago might be designated a "World Heritage Site", but I am far from advocating that! What is clear, I think, is that Orkney is one of the ultimate destinations for cultural tourism, one where mass tourism does not intrude. It is instead a high-quality destination catering for those who wish to explore various aspects of prehistory and history at leisure, while enjoying the natural delights of the landscape.

Photographers and artists also cannot fail to respond to the combination of landscape and old buildings. We do need, however, to ensure that the buildings of each period I have been writing about are valued and protected. The much more recent vernacular buildings, such as the little mills and kilns, are as interesting, as attractive, and as informative as are the chambered tombs.

From the eighteenth century onwards, another style of building appeared briefly in the isles – the elegant classical house that had become very fashionable elsewhere. There are, I think, only three examples, of which two are not in the best of condition. John Rae, the Arctic explorer, was brought up in the Hall of Clestrain, which was built in 1769. Described in the invaluable RIAS volume as "an elegant Georgian mansion", it has lost the shallow pediment that it once probably boasted, and its tall roof looks rather like asbestos sheets. Again, it is in a lovely location, looking across to Hoy. It is important even if only for its connection with Rae. But, as a rare example of a classical house in these northern isles, it certainly deserves to be rescued from decay. Enthusiasts are, I understand, mounting a campaign to save it. Gerramount on Sanday came later, in 1835, and has more detail remaining, but, again sadly, it is roofless. I read that it sat formerly in 100 acres laid out "as a park". (I wish I could know what, in the Orkney landscape, a "park" would look like.) In Kirkwall, Papdale House is, in contrast, inhabited and was visited by Sir Walter Scott. It has a nice, pedimented centre bay.

Eighteen

Christian

When I arrived in Orkney on my first solo visit, my thoughts were entirely dominated by the archaeology that I intended to explore, so even the birds, flowers and landscape took second place. It seems odd to me now that I had so little contact with the inhabitants of the archipelago. But I was a shy boy, and rather kept myself to myself. At the time, I knew, vaguely, that we had family connections with the isles, in that we had Orcadian ancestors. I knew too that my mother had spent a significant amount of time during the Second World War stationed at Hatston, just outside Kirkwall. That war seemed to me, born just four years after it ended, to be the distant past. I recall looking rather askance as I drove up the brae towards the golf course at the shanty-town of Hatston, then to the right of the road. All had been swept away by the time I returned, some twelve years later, with the intention of living and working here.

When we did arrive in Birsay, in the early months of 1980, we had a great deal to do. We had to prepare the rather tired old house for its first guests (a process that took a few winters of painting and reorganising) and get to know the landscape around which I was quite soon to be leading groups of enthusiasts. We did make friends gratifyingly quickly, and got our two girls settled into their new school in Dounby, not that far away. They also enjoyed some of their favourite activities, the most important of which was probably ballet. All of this left little time to explore my family history, but the discovery of that wonderful and detailed tombstone in the Orphir kirkyard encouraged me to look again at the few relevant family papers I had by now been given by my grandmother.

These were really only three, all of which I still have and which are beside me as I write. The most immediate was written by my great-grandmother, Isabel Munro, at a guess some time in the 1930s. It is entitled "Orcadian Descent". I find it interesting, perhaps revealing, that it was she who wrote it, rather than her energetic and practical husband, whose ancestry she was exploring. However, he must at least have provided her with some of the material contained therein. The document, which is fairly easy to read, begins: "This is the pedigree of the Halcrows, or Hacos, who intermarried with the Johnstones." She goes on to refer to a couple of the families later documented in similar terms:

> "The Johnstones are descended from an Earl of Annandale, of the Hope-Johnstone family, who fled to Orkney when in political trouble; and married his first, and lawful, wife there, deserting her on his return to power.
>
> The Robertsons of Struan also fled to Orkney when in political trouble; possibly in the '15, but long before the '45.
>
> These all intermarried over and over again."

While my own rather romantic nature quite enjoyed the thought of this colourful ancestry, I did not fail to notice, when I really began to look at this piece of writing, that Isabel failed to prove any connection between these adventurous families and those of our ancestors whom she later listed. The second and third pages of her manuscript contain a detailed family tree of the ancient Earls of Orkney, starting with "Harold Harfalgar, or Fair-haired, King of Norway, and friend of, and donor of the Earldom of Orkney, to Sigurd, 1st Earl of

Orkney and Shetland". The tree continues down to St Magnus and, nicely, includes the Scandinavian ancestry of William the Conqueror. Once again, however, there is no attempt to link our family with this illustrious background. The same is true of the following page, which includes details of "Clann Donachaidh – (Robertsons)", then a line of descent from Robert the Bruce to "William, Earl of Orkney, Chancellor of Scotland", and an extract from one of the publications of John Mooney (it is not clear whether it is from "Eynhallow, the Holy Isle of the Orkneys" or "Kirkwall in the Orkneys" – both are mentioned).

This section that follows relates to an Erskine family, reputedly of Orcadian descent, one of whom married a Margaret Halcro, and quotes her "Certificate of character from the Kirk Session" (of Evie):

> *"To all and sundry into whose hands these presents shall come, be it known that the bearer thereof, Margaret Halcro, lawful daughter of the deceased Hugh Halcro, in the Isle of Weir, and Margaret Stewart his spouse, hath lived in the Parish of Evie since her infancy, in good fame and report, is a discreet, godly young woman, and, to our certain knowledge, free of all scandal, reproach and blame, and also that she is descended by her father of the House of Halcro, which is a truly ancient and honourable family in the Orkneys – the noble and potent Earl of Early, and the Lairds of Dun in Angus; and by her mother of the Lairds of Barscope, in Galloway."*

This was written in 1666, and signed by "Mr Morisone, Minister, George Ballentine of Evie, James Traill, and William Ballenden". It interests me to see this rather anxious claiming of dim but illustrious ancestry as early as 1666; I am quite accustomed to it from other, generally later, family contexts. Despite her claimed ancestry, I am inclined to the belief that Margaret Halcro lived fairly humbly; I cannot believe that she would otherwise have needed a "Certificate of Character". And, once again, Isabel makes no attempt to detail any connection that the Erskines or Margaret might possibly have to our family.

Accordingly, it was with little reluctance that I set aside these optimistic pages and concentrated on the few that were left. These, helpfully, were straightforward: a tree of the immediate generations of the Munro family into which she had married, and one of her husband's immediate Orcadian connections.

The second document is, in its own way, rather sad, but it is also a rather touching contact from past generations. The key point of contact is Isabel's husband, Donald John Munro, and it is a letter to him from his Orcadian grandmother, dated 24 December 1883, in Stromness. It is very hard to read, and my grandmother Joyce (the daughter of Isabel and Donald John) set herself the task of deciphering it. Sadly, it did not really repay her labour, as the poor old lady's mind was clearly wandering by the time she wrote the letter. It mostly describes her complex network of correspondents (mainly emphasising letters that fail to arrive!), but it appears to make some observations that, if we could but decipher them properly, maddeningly, might be very interesting!

It ends:

Mind let me know, when I will write to meet you. If possible I will have one pair or 2 of socks ready for you. Accept my love,

  From your ever affectionate Grandmother

Ann White

You will (be) surprised to see how I write, now 85 years of age 17 October last.

Although the stated ages and dates do not tally exactly, it is probable that this is the Ann White who is recorded as living as a boarder in the house of John Clouston, Town Crier, in Alfred Street.

I was in the habit by this time of keeping Joyce up to date with my intermittent researches. Finding the above letter prompted the memory that Ann White had latterly been bedridden, and spent her days collecting news from the papers (Lloyds) of where ships were, and their destinations. She then passed the information on to relatives of the crews in Orkney. I guess that, given such reasonably precise information, she would still have been able pass to it on in a more coherent fashion than her letter to Donald John suggests. It is in great contrast to the letters I received from Joyce. She wrote in a most elegant hand, and was clear in what she said up to the very week she died in her ninety-eighth year.

It seemed that Ann must have lived latterly in what used to be called "reduced circumstances", and we always wondered why she had not gone to live with relations. What information we had suggested rather firmly that Ann's own grandmother had ended her days rather differently. That at least was the inference that could be drawn from the third document I brought to Orkney with me.

This document is, as I look at it now, really rather beautiful, comprising no fewer than nine faded, slightly discoloured pages, written closely on both sides. It is a contemporary copy of the "Disposition, Assignation and Settlement by Christian Johnstone, otherways Robertson, to John, Ann, Nicol and James Robertson her children". It was dated 21 September 1826, and each page is countersigned by David Bews, Writer in Kirkwall. Apart from the interest of its content, the will helps to prove the accuracy of the family tree as written by Isabel, although it is interesting that she makes no reference to Christian. And it makes it clear, too, that our family connections are overwhelmingly with the West Mainland, and the four families of

Johnston, Halcro, Robertson and Leith, who were mostly, as one might expect, farmers, with some professionals based in Stromness. Christian's own will makes it clear that the spelling of surnames tended to vary at this period, and both the Johnston and Robertson names, despite Isabel Munro's romantic fancies, almost certainly date back to the days when the patronymic was used; Johnson was the son of John, Robertson the son of Robert and so on. Most of the information we have about these families begins some time in the 1600s or 1700s, and quite a lot of it relates to financial or legal complications, explained perhaps at least in part by the generally prevailing hard times.

We also possess copies of earlier letters from Christian. It is probable that she was descended from other Johnstons on the family tree, who came from Birsay, but I have never proved this. She was certainly born on a large farm there, and was sent south to be educated, which indicates some social and financial standing. She married, in Swannay in December 1795, John Robertson, who was a shipping agent in Stromness and had the four children mentioned above. Her husband died, however, after a long illness in August 1808. Christian wrote a letter in October to her cousins, William and Nicol Leith, in which she said she was "much pinched, owing to a deal of bad debts that is owing my late husband". In 1810, in another letter, it seems clear that things are still bad, and she says "it gives us plenty to do to scrape for a family". She had decided, anyway, to continue to try to run her husband's business in Stromness, and by the time she made her will in 1826, it is clear that she had succeeded very well. She owned a number of ships, some property in Stromness, including the site of the building that for much of my time was the post office, and she built the well-known "Double-houses" on the seafront. These, and the acquisition of a number of properties on the West Mainland, stemmed from the success of her business. Apart from running a few ships herself, she was an agent for, and supplier to, both the Hudson's Bay Company and various whaling concerns. Stromness by this time was a thriving port, often the last call in British waters before crossing the Atlantic to Canada and Greenland. She not only supplied these concerns with critical provisions, but also engaged men on their behalf. She employed in addition a number of women engaged in straw-plaiting, an Orkney cottage industry that flourished for a period. The 1820s were described as "boom years" and Christian's will of 1826 indicates that she did well out of them: at the time, she owned, in addition to the property in Stromness, the land of Greenwall, the farms of Quoykeuan, Ingsay in Birsay, Nistaben in Harray, Lyking above the Loch of Stenness, and the Mill of Ireland, close to Clestrain.

To her daughter, Ann, she left a "cow's grazing on the lands of Greenwall", the "Milnquoy and Mill of Ireland", "with the Multure, Sucken and Sequels of said Miln and Kelp Shores", also "and Whole my tenement of Land or Dwelling House, Quay, Office House and Store House" (which were in Stromness), as well as all her household effects. Had Ann in fact succeeded to this, she would have been relatively well-off, but we do not know what she actually did inherit. The 1830s were poor years in contrast to the preceding decade, and Christian's business may have suffered. Latterly her financial affairs seem complex and she did not find the running of the farms entirely straightforward. She was certainly involved in two legal cases that went to the Court of Session in Edinburgh, and she lost one of them. Despite this, Jim Robertson ('he of the Fudge Factory' according to one of my correspondents), was of the view that Christian had "made the family what it is". (The Robertson name was still prominent in my time, and Robertsons had farmed at Lyking for 200 years.) Christian eventually died in 1835; she was my great-great-great-great-grandmother! Our copy of the 1826 will presumably came down to us via Ann; perhaps she clung to it as a memory of her enterprising mother and what she had achieved.

One small point in particular in the 1826 will was of great interest to me. Christian mentions her only surviving sibling, Magnus, who was now "of Swannay and Tacksman of Boardhouse in the Parish of Birsay" – Boardhouse was the large farm that almost surrounded our house on the Birsay Links. The land around us, the farm adjoining the bay we loved, had belonged to my ancestors. It is a remarkable coincidence, the sort of thing at which the romantic in me rejoiced – but it is also true.

Nineteen

Victorians

By the time that Christian died, overwhelming change was on its way to Orkney. During the preceding century, a mania for agricultural improvement had swept over Scotland, transforming much of the landscape. It was heading for the islands, too, introduced by many of the lairds of the large estates that had been such a prominent feature of Orkney for centuries. I have written something of this elsewhere (*Castles in the Mist*, published by Saraband, 2016), and I will not repeat much here. Suffice it to say that prolonged campaigns saw much of the landscape completely reorganised. The big rectangular fields that are such a feature of today's scene date from this period when the land was drained, ploughed, reseeded, fenced or enclosed by walls, and punctuated by new, solid farmhouses and extensive outbuildings, the occasional "big house" and its fashionable plantation, generally of tough sycamore.

In *Castles in the Mist*, I spent some time on the imposing residences of Balfour and Trumland, both by the noted architect David Bryce, and both worthy of recognition in the wider Scottish context. There are, however, some other Bryce buildings here, and several other substantial houses of the period. I believe that the architectural qualities of Victorian houses in general have been rather ignored, indeed sometimes derided. However, they have an undoubted presence in the island landscape, and their accompanying plantations are important elements in the diversity of the local scenery and habitats.

I used to pass a couple of them on my regular drives from Birsay to Kirkwall. Just after Dounby, the tower and steep roofs of Holodyke are conspicuous on the long agricultural slopes to the north of the main road, and shortly after the junction with the Stromness-Kirkwall road is the big farm of Binscarth, complete with towered farmstead and house, Tudor-style mansion and extensive plantation. These edifices clearly demonstrate the scale of the investment that transformed Orkney around this time.

Orphir, another attractive and rich agricultural district – given relative shelter by hills to the west and north, its smooth fields running down to the gentle coast of Scapa Flow – possesses a remarkable procession of these confident houses. From Houton Bay, heading east, you pass the tall house of Grindally, the tower of Gyre (also called Orphir House because it once functioned as two dwellings – it still has two front stairs), the impressive but slightly plainer Swanbister, and the rather vertical Smoogro (which has an earlier nucleus). In Firth, the Old Manse, which was in my day the home of Liberals Jo and Laura Grimond, was also much enlarged during the nineteenth century.

Considering how windy Orkney is, I am often surprised by the fact that so many of these tall houses stand in prominent positions. Roeberry in South Ronaldsay occupies exactly such a location, on a hilltop overlooking an inlet of the Flow. It has imposing bay windows – remembering the draughts we experienced in our own, much more modest house on the Birsay Links, I can only hope that modern windows have since been fitted. The name here intrigues me, too: I often wonder idly if the element "roe", which is quite common, may conceal the Gaelic "ruadh" for "red", very much the colour of the cliffs below the house.

Several of the remotest Isles can also boast such properties. Holland House in North Ronaldsay is another one with a tower and bay windows, and Hoy contains an extensive but very different group of buildings in Melsetter. This house came much later, being an older house whose transformation was begun by William Lethaby in 1898. It was one of the big houses to which my mother and other Wrens were invited during the last war, and she remembered its very special atmosphere, describing it as "cosy and domestic". She recalled too the rich warmth of the fabrics and carpets by William Morris. Like Balfour, it has its own chapel, and the whole group sits in the farming landscape of South Hoy rather than towering over it. I used to visit another substantial house, Graemeshall in Holm, in order to enjoy the extraordinary collection of antiques it then housed. This too had its own chapel, as well as statues of Faith, Hope and Charity set in the garden wall (and now returned to Inverness, whence they had come).

In Kirkwall, my mother remembered visiting Berstane, another Bryce house. The principal rooms were planned in a similar way to both Balfour and Trumland, although the exterior is very different and is described in the RIAS Orkney guide as a "plain, picturesque villa". She recalled the first floor drawing-room, with its wide sea views. However, the true height of the house is somewhat diminished in appearance by the minimising of the ground floor; it looks altogether more modest than it really is. Another fine house with a splendid view, this time outside Stromness, is Oglaby, owned in those days by another, most hospitable friend.

Orkney had its own distinguished architect during this time, Thomas Smith Peace, who was responsible for a number of houses and many public buildings, most rather baronial in style. The latter included Kirkwall Town Hall, the Kirkwall Hotel, the Masonic hall and the Grammar School (now the offices of Orkney Islands Council), while among his larger houses is Craigiefield. He also built No. 20, High Street (now called Main Street), described as a "low stone pavilion". This, I seem to recall, is where the wonderful Marjory Linklater, widow of the distinguished Orcadian novelist Eric, lived latterly. In Stromness, Peace was responsible for the building that later became the Youth Hostel, in which I occasionally stayed.

Inevitably, with the new agricultural prosperity of the nineteenth century, came the building of many new churches and manses. Some were, of course, in Kirkwall: the Episcopal Church (and Manse) of St Olaf provides another connection with Inverness, as it was the work of the prolific architect Alexander Ross. Among countless other buildings, he was responsible for the Bishop's Palace and Cathedral Church of St Andrew, in their peaceful setting by the broad River Ness (as it happened, this is where my grandmother Joyce was confirmed, married and buried). Not only is this Kirkwall church attractive on the outside, inside it contains a number of interesting relics from the ecclesiastical past of Orkney. The East Church, wonderfully described in the RIAS guide as a "massive, galleried preaching barn", dates, too, from this period of urban expansion, as does the Roman Catholic Church of Our Lady. There are several substantial churches and manses throughout the Orkney countryside, for instance in Harray, where St Michael's Kirk and substantial manse are close to the rival Free Church and its equally fine manse, now called Holland House. Not far away is the house of Dunsyre, another large villa from the same period. Of course, many of the plainer farmhouses also belong to the nineteenth century, and alongside them are found fine farm buildings and several imposing mills. In a number of these, the quality of the masonry is exemplary. I am thinking particularly of a roadside wall at Lyking, and a burnside one beside Tormiston Mill, formerly the Historic Scotland centre for Maeshowe. Some of the mills have been renovated as holiday accommodation or, as in the case of the beautiful buildings of the Mill of Ireland or Eyrland, as a private residence of distinction. This latter is not the structure owned formerly by Christian Robertson, but is one much larger, dating from 1862.

Closer to home, we passed the fine mill complex of Boardhouse almost every day (also called the Barony Mills), which is open to visitors and maintained and run by the Birsay Heritage Trust. The machinery of the period still works, and the interior provides a splendid view into the recent past.

Much more could be said about the built heritage dating from this period. I have not, for instance, referred to the maritime buildings, the piers and jetties, the many storehouses, the fishing-stations, let alone the country schools found all over. I am not suggesting that every single one is of architectural distinction, but together they amount, yet again, to a substantial heritage.

Along with the desire to erect impressive houses in the countryside, there was an intention to transform the nearby landscape into woodland, a truly difficult task in the salt-laden winds of the archipelago. There are now some fine plantations, notably at Binscarth, Gyre, Trumland, Balfour and Woodwick, with smaller examples in a number of other locations. For many decades, these were almost the only sylvan places in Orkney, although the attractive wooded character of much of Finstown was frequently overlooked. Sycamores, faring best in these difficult conditions, were often planted first. The plantations, with their complex, twisting branches, have a very special beauty, particularly of course, in the spring. Another popular tree was the Swedish whitebeam, but within the established shelter of these two species you may find several others, including some conifers, which generally do not flourish here, along with the occasional beech and ash. Others, such as laburnum, appear wonderfully exotic if you wander into the woods from the otherwise pastoral landscape. The primroses (often thought of as a woodland flower) do well in these shady places, but they also grow spectacularly well in the open – frequently on exposed coasts like those of Marwick and Yesnaby. Also growing and blooming abundantly in the plantations are Spanish bluebells. These may be enjoyed without any reservations as there are, I think, none of the native bluebells (*Endymion non-scripta*) here to be threatened by the exotics. The chief beauty of these woods is the springtime carpet of delicate starry flowers ranging from pink to white, the enchanting blossom of the equally exotic plant normally called the pink purslane (*Montia sibirica*). It also grows under some hedges in Orphir, and beside the road at Redland. On a bright day, these are wonderful places, functioning as oases of calm and shelter when the outside world may be swept by strong winds.

The birds, of course, appreciate these surroundings – not just the usual woodland birds such as tits and chaffinches, which are otherwise scarce, but also the rooks and wood-pigeons, which forage during the daytime out in the wide fields. Small migrants frequently take shelter here, and you may hear the constant springtime call of the chiffchaff and willow warbler in the open glades.

After one day on Rousay, I quickly scribbled the following:

"Brilliant sun over water; interlocking shapes of vivid green land and deepest blue water. White of seabird drifts, rich gold of marsh marigold, butter-yellow of primrose in huge clumps that strain upwards to the sun. Through Trumland woods; new leaves of green, pink-green, white-green, lemon-green, silver-green; bright-dotted carpet of pink (Montia sibirica), cool blue richness of glades of bluebell, trembling ballerina-flowers of fuchsia coming in the lush hedges. Who could forget such a day?"

The Victorians transformed Orkney, and left an inheritance that was far more than simply big fields, fine farms and strong houses. Their plantations can ease the soul after a hard winter. Rather wonderfully, their example is now being followed by many Orcadians, who are now adding to the diversity of the island environment.

Twenty

Arctic Connections

When we were living in Orkney, we spent quite a lot of time going to Stromness. This was partly because it was where we obtained a significant amount of our supplies and partly because most of our guests would arrive there on the ferry. When I first arrived in my little Morris Minor this had been the *St Ola*. "Meeting the *Ola*" became such a constant routine, that I still find myself misnaming the current very different ferry, which has done the route for countless years and is called after the original name of the little port, hence the *Hamnavoe*. The name "Stromness" properly refers to the Ness or headland to its south, off which there often run very strong currents and tides, the "strom" of the name.

It has often seemed very odd to me that, apparently, until the seventeenth century there were only a few cottages and huts on the shores of the sheltered voe under the hill of Brinkie's Brae. One would have expected at least a fishing village there, but there was little development until ships started heading much further north and west, across the Atlantic, and Stromness became the last victualling and watering stop in British waters.

The simple family tree that Isabel Munro had outlined, that of her husband Donald John's Orcadian forebears (the real ones, rather than the legendary connections), provided me with the names of those ancestors, but it is always nice to learn more about the individuals concerned. As has been seen, this was fairly easily done in the case of my great-great-great-great-grandmother, Christian Robertson, but, rather paradoxically, it proved more difficult with her descendants. There was some confusion between what my grandmother had said and her father had written, so there are some individuals about whom we are less certain. In part, at least, this is because one set of grandfather, father and son all had the same name (Thomas White), and the second Thomas's wife and daughter were both christened Ann – although to try to minimise any confusion, the younger was often called Annie. Both the first two Thomases were sometimes described as "shipmaster", with the second often being referred to as "Captain". And the connection with the Arctic and the Hudson's Bay Company certainly continued, so Stromness remained an important base for the family.

Of the first Thomas White we know only a little. But we do know he was a very lucky young man. In 1980, I wrote to James Halcro Johnston at Orphir House, asking for any relevant information, and, in reply, he sent the following extract from a letter dated May 1884, from James Johnston to his son, Alfred W. Johnston : "Thomas White, Shipmaster, Stromness, married Jean Johnston, 5th daughter of Joshua Johnston and Margaret Halcro. He was one of three saved of twenty-two young men from Stromness, 19 lost on a pleasure trip to Sule Skerry (William Halcro, the heir to the estate of Coubister, was one of them)." Another account states that Thomas was actually rescued "off the North Faro Isles". I only wish we knew more about this pleasure trip that went so drastically wrong, why or how Thomas and two others survived, and how they eventually managed to get home to Stromness. Despite his youthful luck, we think that Thomas was eventually lost at sea, but before that happened, he and Jean had had at least one child, the son they (less than helpfully) also called Thomas, born around 1797.

Donald John described the second Thomas, who was nearly always called "Captain Thomas White", as a "privateer", and I went to the dictionary to check what this implied. Such an individual is described as "the commander of an armed vessel owned and officered by private individuals holding a government commission and authorised for war service". More often, such a person is described as "a licensed pirate", so one of my direct ancestors was very nearly a pirate – how I would have enjoyed knowing that when I was a little boy! The manner in which he became part of the family was told both by Jim Robertson and by Donald John in one of his books (of which, more, later). It was said that Thomas White had sailed into Stromness one day and invited the Provost of the burgh (who was Christian's brother) and some members of the family, including Ann, to lunch on board, along with the local minister. Later in the day, perhaps after a good meal, he stated that he was going to up-anchor and sail immediately for the West Indies, with the whole party on board, unless Ann agreed to marry him at once, which in fact she did. It is almost certain that this was something of a "put-up job", as there was family disapproval of the proposed match. Ann would have counted as quite an heiress (under her mother's will of 1826), and a privateer might not, perhaps, have been the sort of man thought suitable by her extended family.

Be that as it may, the marriage seems to have prospered, initially at least, and when Thomas and Ann next came to Stromness, it was with an infant daughter. The child, also called Ann (born, we think, around 1827), was left in the care of the childless Provost, Bailie John Robertson, and his wife, her great-uncle and -aunt. Ann senior is said to have sailed with her husband for some years, but must have returned by 1841 when she is again resident in Stromness. But noticeably, she did not live with her children at Ness. Was there some estrangement within the family? It would certainly explain why, even in old age, she did not go to live with her daughter. (But that would have been to a location she did not know, on the far west coast of the Scottish mainland.)

Quite where she sailed with her husband, and what exactly he was up to, is far from clear. He was variously credited with captaining a merchant ship owned by the East India Company, another vessel called the *Endeavour*, and one of which Jim Robertson had a retouched photo, reproduced here. He claimed it was of "the *Meta* which belonged to the Moravian Missionary Society, in Stromness Harbour in 1866, and bound for Labrador, under the command of Captain Thomas White". I feel that the date, at least, must be quite wrong, as Thomas White would by then have been almost seventy years old. In addition, it is believed that he went with one of the expeditions to look for traces of the unfortunate Franklin expedition, whose ships had watered in Stromness in 1845.

The first overland search for the Franklin party was initiated in 1848, led by Sir John Richardson and John Rae, while ship-borne searches (more likely to have included Thomas White) began in 1850. In 1855, yet another effort involved men from the Hudson's Bay Company, and again this may have included Orcadians. If Thomas White had been involved in any of these, it seems quite unlikely he would have been in command of any ship in 1866. In any case, my grandmother was convinced that he was lost in one of the searches.

With his daughter, generally known as Annie, we are on slightly more secure ground, at least for much of her life. She was definitely born in 1827, and certainly raised by her great uncle and aunt of whom she remained, according to my grandmother, extremely fond. They paid for her later education in Edinburgh, at one of the Merchant Company Schools, but it is not clear at what age she would have left that school. I'm curious about this because there is a very real gap in our knowledge of Ann Johnston(e) White between her time at school in Edinburgh and her marriage, at the age of very nearly thirty-two, to Hector Munro, who had quite recently joined the Excise Preventive Service and was living at that point in London. In fact, we have no official record of what Hector had been doing either, for at least the previous decade!

According to my grandmother (his granddaughter, who knew him well), he must have left school around the age of fourteen, at the latest sixteen. He joined the Hudson's Bay Company, which would have meant, almost definitely, passing through Stromness on occasion, probably getting to know people there – maybe even the girl he would eventually marry. He certainly had some adventures in the Arctic. I quote one letter from Joyce, written when she was about ninety-five, in a very legible handwriting: "He had been out there for a few years, and on one occasion he set out with his sledge of huskies to set up a new station. But very bad weather set in, blinding snow and a cruel wind. The dogs died one by one – except one. They carried on, no food or shelter. Grandfather carried the remaining dog in his arms, until suddenly the dog lifted his head and sniffed the air over his shoulder; so they turned slightly and came on an Indian (Eskimo?) encampment, and that saved them both. I remember my grandfather telling me this one day when we were sitting beside the mill stream at Auchindoune." (This house, near Cawdor, was later the family home for three generations.)

As would be expected, after marrying Hector (in a church in the Old Kent Road, of all unlikely places!), her life followed his. His career took him around the Highlands, being based first of all in Poolewe, then Fort Augustus, subsequently at Greenfield in Glen Garry and ultimately in Gairloch. During this time, she had four children. The first, a daughter, was born in Stromness, in 1860; she was given the names Margaret Robertson, and the birth was registered by her uncle, so the Orkney connection clearly remained strong. Later sons were christened Donald John and Hector, very much Munro names, and the other daughter, Grace.

We know that both boys at least were at first educated locally, then sent to Inverness Royal Academy for a year or two, although Donald John certainly left school at fourteen to go to sea. Whether this was an initiative of Annie's – because she herself had been sent to school in Edinburgh – we do not know, but I am very much inclined to see something of her influence in what they did when Hector reached retirement age. At this point, when they could presumably have acquired a modest house somewhere and settled down to a quiet old age, they went, instead, into farming in quite a serious way. They took on the tenancy of Auchindoune (mentioned above), quite a substantial farm and dignified old house that had formerly been (as it again now is) the Dower House of the Cawdor Estates. Soon after, they purchased a small sheep farm on the West Coast, that of Glen More near Lochcarron. I find it hard to believe that this could all be done on savings from Hector's pay as a minor sort of civil servant, so I imagine that Annie by this time might well have inherited money from her childless relatives in Stromness. Wherever the impetus came from, Auchindoune remained a much-loved focus for the family until 1928; my mother had the faintest recollection of going there as a very small child.

Twenty-one

The Making of the Sailor

It could fairly be said, perhaps, that the Victorians laid the foundations of modern Orkney (although if I were being purist, I would argue that the real foundation is, in fact, the geology). The nineteenth century certainly saw Orkney transformed and brought into line in so many ways with much of the rest of non-industrial Britain. The first half of the twentieth century once again saw Orkney play a part in the front line of conflict, this time on a world scale, and, as it happens, members of my family were involved. One of them actually had, through his First World War work, an importance that is hard to exaggerate.

This was Donald John, elder son of Annie Johnston Munro, nee White, of Stromness. Although he was brought up in the Highlands and was a fluent Gaelic speaker, it is apparent that he spent holidays in Stromness, presumably on the farm at Ness (I think where the golf course is now), in the Robertson household. It also seems that he took to boating like a duck to water. There could hardly be a better place: Hamnavoe offered calm, sheltered water, while the channel across to Hoy would often show the might of the sea, a reminder of why it should always be respected.

At the age of fourteen, Donald John went to sea, like so many of his forebears, and he later wrote up the story of his voyages on sailing-ships, and subsequently in the River Police in Burma. This book, *The Roaring Forties and After*, is certainly full of adventure and death-defying scrapes. It might be described as a "rattling good yarn" were his style not so calm and dispassionate – there are several moments when I want to interrupt him and ask: "Yes, but what did it actually feel like?" It is too late for me to find that out now, but it is clear that Donald John excelled at almost everything he undertook. By the time he was nineteen, he was in charge of a boat on one of the great rivers of Burma, at times under fire, and responsible for the lives of others.

There is no space here to record his early adult life in detail. While in India, he met his future wife, Isabel, and it may have been this that inspired him to return first of all to the Merchant Navy, and subsequently to take advantage of a scheme by which senior men of the mercantile marine might transfer to the Royal Navy. His second book begins with the following paragraph: "My appointment on 25th November, 1904, as Assistant King's Harbour Master and Assistant to the Commander of H M Dockyard, Sheerness, proved to be a momentous one in my career."

The first line of the second paragraph is crucial: "It placed me in immediate contact with the naval developments taking place on the East Coast of England and Scotland." While it is clear that Donald John was immensely practical, both as a seaman and later as a farmer (therefore, very much an Orcadian in spirit), he was also a very independent thinker. He began, in this new posting, to consider the implications of the beginning, at that time, of the great build-up in strength of the German navy, and the inevitability of conflict with Britain. In fact, DJ's work took him right up the East Coast, and he was able to see for himself the condition of the various harbours that would have a vital role to play in the event of war. Much had been made of the new class of battleships, the Dreadnoughts, which the British navy had introduced with great pride, but DJ noted that there was literally only one dry dock that could accommodate such a ship. He remarks: "It was unfortunate that those responsible for the introduction of a new type of capital ship did not realise that either old dry docks must be altered, or new ones built, before the new fleet of Dreadnoughts could be efficient." Although, as he says, "in a very junior position", he began at this stage to show the very great determination he possessed, both to think things out clearly and to put forward his carefully considered and always practical solutions. "I still stuck to my guns, but with little or no success" … "The whole position occupied my earnest attention, and my mind became focussed on the question of suitable harbours on the East Coast from which great fleets could act" … "It became obvious that there were only three to be seriously considered, the Firth of Forth, Cromarty, and Scapa." Underlying this practical interest was his belief that war, when it came, would "prove a long drawn out affair and all arrangements should be based on this assumption".

By 1907, he was delivering lectures on the state of the relevant harbours, and all the practicalities of various kinds of dock. While I can imagine that these lectures were quite heavy-going for the average listener, he began to catch the ear of at least one very senior figure, the new Controller of the Admiralty, Admiral Jellicoe, and he soon found himself lecturing to senior naval officers at the new War College. This gave him the encouragement he needed to continue to think out the solutions to practical problems, and then to communicate his answers to these problems to the Lords Commissioners of the Admiralty. From here he initiated a flood of precisely detailed common-sense arrangements and improvements to accepted practice that continued until well after he had officially retired. These covered, for instance, the important topic of mine-sweeping, and one area that would prove crucial to his career – and the safety of the British Fleet itself when war did come – the boom defence. He also began at this stage to take out, on behalf of the navy, secret patents, mostly related to improvements he devised to articles of use such as otter boards, which were used in mine-sweeping operations.

The idea of a boom defence was hardly new; the notion of stretching a very strong rope or chain across a narrow opening, in order to block it, had apparently been used in classical Greece. It certainly appears in Highland mythology at places such as Kyleakin. The problems faced by the British navy in the lead-up to the Great War were, however, rather more complex – and urgent – as they faced a new weapon against which they had no effective defence: the U-boat. A modern boom defence would have to be very strong and it would have to fit the underwater contours, as far as possible, of the channel where it was to be placed. It would also, of course, have to open to allow ships to pass through. Given the strong currents found in many such channels, these were daunting requirements, and DJ found that "there was no proposal or plan existent to resist the entrance of underwater craft". He therefore decided that something had to be done, and succeeded in persuading the Admiralty to set up a committee. This was effected (although there were many weaknesses in the way it was organised), but he was at least a member of that committee. Trials of various designs began, although the initial results were not exactly encouraging. One of the main problems was that no practical surface boom, if its ends were rigidly secured, could possibly withstand the impact of a destroyer weighing 600 tons and travelling at 35 knots. But DJ's very practical curiosity provided the answer. He happened one day to see an oil tanker, the *Iroquois*, towing the *Navahoe*, a very large barge, and he wondered exactly how they effected this. He managed to get himself on board, and thus was introduced to the American towing winch, which ultimately provided the required solution. Successful tests included one crucial one, before the First Lord of the Admiralty, Winston Churchill, and Admiral Jellicoe, individuals whose support would be invaluable to him in the future.

There remained, however, the tricky question of underwater protection. The chairman of the committee did not believe it was within their remit, and would take no steps to get that remit widened. In the meantime, Commander Munro, as DJ now was, was in 1911 transferred to Scotland, appointed Senior Naval Officer and King's Harbour Master at Rosyth on the Forth Estuary. Before he left to take up the post, he was interviewed by the First Sea Lord, who impressed on him the importance of an immediate examination of the state of the Firth of Forth, as the prospect of war, at least in Churchill's mind, loomed closer. The first inspection revealed that the great estuary was almost totally unprepared and unprotected, and Munro's report was followed, in time, by a visit from the Secretary of State for War, who was apparently non-committal. Perhaps fortunately, that visit was followed by one by Churchill. This resulted in DJ producing a memorandum on the state and requirements of all the East Coast harbours, in which, among many other items, he stressed the natural advantages of the Cromarty Firth. This was the first of a crucial series of discussions, letters and memoranda that continued for a considerable time between DJ and Churchill, without any intermediary. Consequently, serious and urgent attention was given to the defence of these harbours. As a result of these exchanges, and the relative simplicity of proposed operations at Cromarty, it was decided that "Cromarty was to be taken in hand at once", with DJ appointed SNO and King's Harbour Master there, as well as Executive Officer of the small committee appointed to oversee the work. The committee acted promptly: plans were drawn up and approved, which, it was estimated, would take a year to complete. It was now July 1913.

The important work of defending the spacious harbour of the Cromarty Firth was undertaken with great energy on the part, it would seem, of all concerned. DJ was clearly in his element and no doubt supplied much of the driving force behind the project, as well as a lot of the practical vision required to get things done at speed. A clear example of this lay in the installation of the heavy (9.2-inch) guns that were to be mounted on the two prominent headlands, the Souters, which guard the entrance to the Firth. The guns were landed on the respective beaches, but between those points and their final destinations on the heights, lay inadequate roads, with a gradient of one in four at one point, some three miles of travel and an ascent of around 500 feet. The War Office, tied to traditional ideas, decided the best way to move the guns would be by "means of tackle and capstan", which they estimated would take some weeks. Commander DJ Munro used traction engines and had them in place within three days. They also mounted searchlights on the cliffs, to illuminate at night the single entrance to the spacious harbour, laid electric and telegraph cables, built small underground power stations, smaller gun batteries, magazines and barracks. While all this was in progress, Churchill visited with the First Sea Lord, Prince Louis of Battenberg (later Mountbatten), as did the Prime Minister, Mr Asquith. Later, when the big guns came to be calibrated, thus preparing them for action, Churchill again visited and watched the operation. My grandmother, Joyce, who must have been approaching eighteen on this occasion, was with her father. He appeared to her to be quizzing Churchill on when he expected war to break out. She vividly remembered him saying: "Sooner than you think, Munro, sooner than you think", and she noticed the look on her father's face. He was clearly making up his mind about something.

In the meantime, the Admiralty was not exactly covering itself in glory. Once the defence of Cromarty was accomplished, it had been the intention that the same committee should take on the much greater challenge of defending Scapa Flow. However, after plans had been drawn up, the idea was cancelled and the money spent instead on work on the breakwater at Dover Harbour. In addition, it was announced that no further work on boom defences would be undertaken by the committee to which it had been entrusted. I have no idea what DJ said when he heard of these pieces of idiocy, but it very clearly strengthened his iron resolve to complete the fortification of the Firth in a way that had hardly even been discussed, and he doubted would ever be authorised. In other words, he intended to protect the harbour against submarine attack. Accordingly, he laid his plans, and as soon as war was declared, on 4 August 1914, Donald John went into action on a very broad front.

As all communication with the Admiralty and anyone else went through the local public telegraph office, and DJ was about to initiate work of national urgency, he took over and moved the office itself. Through it, he ordered a number of vessels: tugs, lighters, harbour launches and puffers, while ensuring that the floating dock and crane that he had been trying to secure for the base for months were at last on their way. This was a journey itself infinitely more risky than it would have been only a little before. He also ordered significant volumes of material, including wood, wire ropes and winches, commandeered trawlers, requested key personnel, took over a boat yard in Inverness, and started work on his first boom in the basin of the Caledonian Canal. All this he did entirely without higher authority, but he worked so fast that it seems to have taken the Admiralty some time to catch up with what was going on.

In his book, he remarks: "The work of laying the moorings, fitting up the trawlers, and building the sections of the boom complete with (hanging) net, went on apace and simultaneously." Nowhere, though, does he mention the extraordinary feats of practical marine design, organisation and seamanship required in the work of effectively hanging gates across the channel that gives access to the Cromarty

Firth, every detail of which he oversaw. Everyone got swept up in the work – small wonder that the members of the Council of the Clan Munro (Association) that he later helped to found in the "leisure" years of his retirement used to call him "Hurricane Jack" behind his back! His two daughters found themselves involved in the war effort, too, splicing wire hawsers (for the boom nets) on the Thornbush Quay in Inverness. (Quite what his rather delicate wife, Isabel, thought of this activity for the young ladies she was trying to rear, is, sadly, not recorded.)

The work had been initiated on 5 August; the first section of the boom was in place by 15 October and the final section by 26 October. The Cromarty Firth, at this date, was the first and only harbour in the world to be securely defended from submarine attack.

DJ had ensured that he had kept the "Commander-in-Chief of the Grand Fleet" (at the time, I think, this must have been Jellicoe) in touch with what he was doing. The latter arrived to inspect it on the day of its completion and "was very satisfied with it". This was probably just as well, as the following day, a telegram from the Admiralty arrived: "It is understood Commander Munro, King's Harbour Master, has constructed and placed in position an anti-submarine defence in the entrance to Cromarty Firth. This officer is to immediately forward... his reasons and by whose authority this work has been carried out."

According to DJ, he promised to try to place his motives on paper, but because of the continuing work had not managed to do so by the next day, when a further telegram arrived summoning him to report immediately to the Fourth Sea Lord at the Admiralty. This entailed a long journey by night train from Inverness. Even he, I suspect, was a trifle unsure what his reception would be, as there was no doubt he had completely bypassed all the "usual channels", an action hardly likely to elicit the approval of the top brass. As it happened, he met the Fourth Sea Lord (whom he knew from past days) in a passage, and later recounted: "Taking me by the arm he announced that I was about to incur their Lordship's displeasure for placing a boom across Cromarty Firth without asking their approval, but that they had instead promoted me to Captain." During the long meeting that followed, Munro was placed in charge of the defence of all the harbours, with Scapa Flow being accorded the highest priority. On his return to Cromarty, he permitted himself one of his few reflective moments:

"It was with deep regret that I surrendered my charge of Cromarty.

Motoring along the high ridge dividing the harbour from the Moray Firth, I beheld this noble port bathed in moonlight with a mighty fleet lying peacefully at anchor and more dimly the floating dock where a glare told of the docking work in progress.

On the twin headlands behind me the flashing of numerous searchlights proclaimed the ceaseless vigil over the open sea.

It was indeed a curious chain of circumstances which led me when a boy to leave this district and spend thirty-four years roaming the seven seas; to be led back again by slow stages from Sheerness to Rosyth, and thence to Cromarty (the home of my fathers) and finally to Scapa (that of my mother). Thus to become the chief agent in the defence of these two ports, now containing between them the most powerful fleet ever assembled to defend these islands; and on which also depended the destinies of the greatest Empire the world has ever seen."

In this lofty and determined mood, Captain Donald John Munro embarked on the greatest challenge of his adventurous life, the fortification of the crucial harbour of Scapa Flow.

Twenty-two

Scapa Flow

If you were to divide the archipelago into North and South, as war-ring Earls had sometimes done, Scapa Flow would be the centre of the southern half. To describe it as a "sheltered deep-water harbour" might raise eyebrows among those who know it well, because the shelter, provided by the gentle hills of Orphir and the higher ones of Hoy, is strictly relative. I recall one description of the Flow being the only place where one could easily encounter "a seventy mile-an-hour fog". However, it is relatively sheltered, and, importantly, it lacks the armoured shore of Orkney, the long cliffs that face out to sea.

It is a large area of water, the second largest such harbour in the British Isles I have read, and you can spend quite a lot of time driving round its shores. The best views of its wide expanse are found where the roads gain a little height. From Stromness itself you do not see much of it, but if, once past the Brig o' Waithe, you take the road for Orphir, past the Mill of Ireland and Hall of Clestrain, the road gains height under the Hill of Midland, and above the Bay of Houton. Here the view is excellent – on a fine day, of course! Along the coast of Orphir itself, the road to Kirkwall is set back among the lush fields, although the little road to the Round Church takes you closer. Nearer Kirkwall, again the road gains some height, and you can look across the head of the Flow, Scapa Bay itself, with its sweep of sand. Heading into Holm, the road past the Highland Park distillery gives you another version of the same view, and you can appreciate (more easily, perhaps, on the return journey) why Kirkwall has grown up where it is. The isthmus between Scapa and Kirkwall Bay is narrow, an obvious portage for Viking longships, and a nodal point for land-based communication.

From here, the road runs a bit inland, but there are good views southwards before you dip down to the village of St Mary's, and cross Lamb Holm and Glims Holm, almost at sea-level now, en route to the larger isles of Burray and South Ronaldsay. Absolutely the best views are to be had if you take the road through the little village of St Margaret's Hope ("Hope", or "Ob", is a bay, and this is a fine little harbour within the much greater), wending your way out to the former island of Hoxa. Passing the storm beaches which link the two, you head up and over the little "island" where, at one point, the houses by the narrow road have taken over the verges and beautifully planted them. As you reach the crest of the hill (en route to the wonderful Tapestry Gallery which I have previously mentioned, and an unexpected and excellent tearoom), almost the full extent of Scapa Flow is before you.

The other way to experience the Flow is, of course, on the water. I have only done this by ferry; from Stromness to Mo Ness in Hoy, passing the small isle of Graemsay, from Houton to Lyness, and, once, to the terminal on Flotta. The route to Lyness goes past the even smaller isles of Cava, Rysa and Fara, all now unpopulated. I have always believed that these windswept small islands give the Flow its name; the Firth of bald, or scalped, islands. It certainly looks appropriate from the water.

Although fierce currents, serious tides, rocks and shoals provided some sort of natural protection, in its undefended state and despite its strategic position between the North Sea and the Atlantic Ocean, at the outset of war Scapa Flow was not exactly the safe anchorage the Grand Fleet needed. Much later there were several descriptions of the problem, but perhaps the most authoritative came from Admiral Lord Jellicoe, in his book *The Grand Fleet*, where he writes:

> "As is well known, the Grand Fleet was moved to Scapa Flow during the latter days of July, 1914, and the defenceless condition of the base, both against destroyer attack and submarine attack, was brought very strongly into prominence, by the presence of so valuable a fleet at this base.
>
> Consequently, the anxiety of officers in command of the Fleet of squadrons at anchor in any of the bases used by the Grand Fleet was immense. For my part, I was always far more concerned for the safety of the Fleet when it was at anchor in Scapa Flow during the exceedingly brief periods which were spent there for coaling in the early days of the war, than I was when the Fleet was at sea.
>
> It was also the cause of my taking the Fleet to sea very hurriedly on more than one occasion owing to the reported presence of a submarine in the anchorage, and considerable risks were accepted in getting the Fleet to sea in very thick weather [a seventy mile-an-hour fog?] at night, on at least one of these occasions."

In short, the Grand Fleet, on which so much depended, had no safe base, and this was the problem which Donald John came north to solve.

Some work had already been initiated to close the eastern channels into the Flow, as well as the channel between Hoy and Graemsay, and this was continued. This was done by what appears as the simple expedient of sinking the hulls of old naval and mercantile ships across the channels, but this task was, in fact, far from simple, and required considerable seamanship; manoeuvring the hulks close together until they virtually touched was tricky enough, but as the

177

gap narrowed, the erosive power of the tidal currents dramatically increased making the task of achieving the final closure significantly more difficult. DJ was no believer in half measures (a critical point to remember in connection with events at the outset of the next war), and the blockships between Holm and Burray were supplemented by the fixture of a permanent closed boom to the west, while the islet of Hunda was eventually connected by a solid causeway.

This left the huge task of positioning his opening booms across the three main entrances of Hoxa Sound, (from where booms ran across to Flotta), Switha Sound, with booms between Flotta and South Walls of Hoy, and between Graemsay and the Mainland coast south of Clestrain. (This allowed the Fleet good access both to the south and to the west.) This was an enormous venture, requiring great quantities of supplies which had to be brought a considerable distance, all during the worst weather that a northern winter could produce. He records "On one occasion the wind blew at over 100 miles per hour. This, with the short days and high seas set up, made life for officers and men very strenuous. It was seaman's work pure and simple, and no-one but a seaman in every sense of the word was any use".

These defences were complete in June, 1915, and, while shore-based gun emplacements were being completed, old battleships were moored up at each entrance to render some sort of protection. Thus protected, Scapa remained a safe base for the operations of the Grand Fleet throughout the years of the war, and it was because of its size and security that it is there that the captured German fleet was taken at the end of hostilities. The pattern of boom defence, devised at Cromarty, and seriously tried and tested in Scapa, was repeated all round the coast of Britain, and I have been informed by American visitors interested in naval history, that it was in use in the Pacific during the Second World War.

It was also largely from Scapa that the Grand Fleet set out for that great, indecisive engagement known as the Battle of Jutland; Orkney was the centre for its commemoration in 2016, (the year during which I wrote this), one hundred years later. And that same year, the Hampshire left the Flow with Kitchener on board, only to come to grief in Birsay Bay.

Joyce, Donald John's eldest daughter, accompanied her father back to Scapa in 1920, but during the years of the War, her life, like that of so many others, had been drastically changed. She was by now 24, had been married and tragically widowed after only a few months, just before the Armistice. Ostensibly, she recovered from this, but when she married again, some years later, it was to a man with a startling physical resemblance to her dead soldier. He was, however, of a very different character, and it was not a marriage that prospered. For one thing, he was tone deaf and quite uninterested in music, while she was musical, a singer and violin player of concert standard. As with so many millions of people, the war had changed her life and things were never quite the same.

But she remembered that visit with her father very clearly. Two aspects of it, in particular, stayed with her into great old age. They had driven up to Thurso and taken the boat to Stromness where they were staying, but went out into the Flow a couple of times. The few Germans left on their captured ships had, as is well known, been determined that they would not be used by the victorious Allies, and had succeeded in scuttling them. The area where they had been moored (and where you may today see boats involved in the diving of the wrecks, which has become a significant visitor activity), is pretty well on the passage from Houton to Lyness, to the north of Rysa and Cava. According to Joyce "one could only see their masts at high water, but at low tide they were half exposed". Interestingly, she goes on to remark that the "locals had proceeded to help themselves to anything they could possibly remove" – which is precisely what one would expect; shades of "Whisky Galore" but in another island context, and slightly less romantic!

Joyce and her father were staying in the dignified Stromness Hotel, and had been intrigued by a number of wooden cases along the hotel landings and corridors. On one occasion, she had been sitting in the lounge, when a man came in. His features strongly reminded Joyce of her grandmother, Annie, and when her father came in she mentioned it to him. He went over and the two men joined in discussion for a time, before inviting Joyce to join them. It turned out that the stranger was a cousin of Annie's, a Colonel Henry Halcro Johnston, who was at that time residing in the hotel. He would have been 62 then, having had a distinguished career as an army surgeon in Sudan, in India, and during the Boer War. He had retired in 1913, only to re-join when war broke out a year later, when he worked as Director of Medical Services in Glasgow, then in York, and finally in Gibraltar. Now properly in retirement, he was living in the hotel, and the cases on the landings were his. A keen and thorough botanist, he was keeping his specimens in them.

A letter from my grandmother, written when she was well into her 90s, records this meeting and adds, rather intriguingly "He had all the fishermen organised to find plants on the cliffs for him, I believe he collected many plants never found in Orkney before". I suppose this might, perhaps, refer to plants growing on the high cliffs of Hoy, which are actually surprisingly well-vegetated, and, on rare calm days might be accessible from a lobster-boat, exactly of the type which another Orcadian, Stanley Cursiter, so often painted in later life. His studies as an artist were also interrupted by the war, and he, too, had a distinguished military career, despite being inva-lided out after the horrific conditions in the trenches had made him ill. I read that he later transferred to the 4th Field Ordnance Survey

Battalion, where he was responsible for devising a much faster method of locating enemy gun emplacements from aerial photographs – another Orcadian with enormous talents for the practical, whose skill was of almost incalculable benefit to the great, national, wartime effort.

Twenty-three

Orcadian Artists

The nineteenth century in Orkney was about much more than new methods of farming and big new houses. It saw the beginning of what might even be called an Orcadian Renaissance, with an explosion of education, creativity, investigation and publication in numerous fields of activity, and this continued into the early twentieth century, with Orcadian names beginning to be known throughout Britain, or even further afield. The First World War cut across the careers of most if not all of them, but they often went on to flourish in the twenty-one years of peace which followed.

One of the earlier Orcadian writers to become quite widely known is generally now referred to as Storer Clouston, although he was usually called "Joe", apparently, from Joseph, his first name. He had wide interests; he trained as a lawyer but never practised, investigated and excavated many island sites, wrote a fine history of Orkney and a number of popular novels, some of which drew on his Viking ancestry. His home was Smoogro, one of the tall houses in Orphir which overlook the Flow.

Another, later Orcadian who made his name as a novelist was Eric Linklater; he survived a bullet wound in the Great War, and used his experiences of trench warfare in a couple of subsequent books. He travelled widely between 1925 and 1930, but by then his literary career had blossomed. He was a prolific writer and his novels, some again with Viking themes, enjoyed great success for a number of years. While his sales may have diminished latterly, it is fair to say that the depth and scope of his writing increased. No doubt partly inspired by his own return to active military service in the Second World War, he explored issues raised by war, the distinctions between nationalism and a sense of national identity, as well as history and autobiography. He died in 1974, and was survived for many years by his lively, attractive and influential wife, Marjorie, whom I knew quite well during my Orkney years.

Marjorie was prominent in the founding of the St Magnus Festival, and responsible for many years for an important part of it, the Johnsmas Foy, described as a "showcase for Orkney literature and folklore". Possibly her greatest contribution to Orkney as we know it today was her campaign against the mining of uranium in the islands, which was favoured by the Westminster Government of the day, led by Margaret Thatcher. Marjorie also chaired the Orkney Heritage Society, and raised funds towards the founding of the post of County Archaeologist, which initiated the first, systematic approach to the islands' astonishing heritage of ancient buildings.

She was also very interested in the visual arts, a field where another Orcadian had made his name, Stanley Cursiter. He was a splendid painter, still I think much neglected south of the Border, a man who abandoned "modern art" when he returned to civilian life in Edinburgh. Perhaps influenced by his work as keeper of the National Portrait Gallery and subsequently, Director of the National Gallery, he reverted to a more traditional style, one to which he brought enormous sensitivity and great technical skill. Among many portraits, he painted one of Marjorie (looking surprisingly demure), and another of Eric, but I think I prefer the astoundingly beautiful still lifes, like those of white china or red lacquer bowls.

He and his Orcadian wife retired to Stromness, where they converted the lovely Stenigar, a much-admired house in which boats had previously been built. He painted many island land- and seascapes; a favourite subject was Yesnaby, which later would have been the location for the uranium mining that Marjorie had helped prevent. In his day, as now, it was a lovely spot, but there were noticeably many more boats drawn up then on the one shingle beach which breaches the canted cliffs.

Stanley had attended Kirkwall Grammar School, where one of his contemporaries was Edwin Muir. They were friends, despite the significant difference in their circumstances. Stanley's family was exceedingly prosperous, while Edwin's were poor farmers who had moved around, from Deerness to Wyre and thence to the Orkney Mainland. Ultimately, they abandoned the islands and the young Edwin went with them to live in what was then the urban and industrial squalor of Glasgow, where in the space of very few years, his parents and his two brothers died. For the young boy from the islands, these experiences were deeply traumatic. He came to think of Orkney as an unspoiled Eden, in contrast to the "fallen" world which he now inhabited and where he had to do some grim work in order to feed himself. He was saved when he met and married Willa Anderson, according to him "the most fortunate event in his life", and they moved to London, the beginning of an academic collaboration and highly mobile life together. He spent a lot of time in Europe, but was also for a period, Warden of Newbattle Abbey College, outside Edinburgh, to which George Mackay Brown would come.

Edwin's own poetry avoids any hint of gimmick, modern experiment or "flashiness", and it is probably fair to say that it attracted nothing like the attention which it really deserves. It is not, in fact, that easy to read, or so I find, despite its apparent simplicity. Edwin was obviously very well read (a tribute, if one were needed, to Kirkwall Grammar School), and deeply intellectual. That he was highly regarded by his peers is indicated by the fact that Kathleen

Raine wrote a review of his collected poems for the New Statesman, and T S Eliot a preface to the Faber selection which he had edited, and which I acquired not long after my arrival in Orkney. In that slim volume, there are very few poems which are obviously Orcadian in inspiration, and one, called "The Island", was actually written about Sicily.

There is one, "There's nothing here" which purports to be a soliloquy by Edwin Muir's cousin Sutherland, awaking after death to find himself in heaven. That poem, I think, speaks for itself and its Orkney background.

To another in that collection, T S Eliot ascribed two adjectives; "great" and "terrifying". It is called "The Horses" and begins:

Barely a twelvemonth after
The seven days' war that put the world to sleep,
Late in the evening the strange horses came.

I never doubted that the setting of the poem is Orkney, seen not necessarily as some Eden, but as a place where a rural sanity will somehow prevail after world disaster. I tried then to create something visual from the words, a triptych which was clearly set in the island landscape. It did not work, as the final two pictures lacked the spontaneity of the first, which represented the moment of the arrival of the horses. I still have that one, and despite its obvious shortcomings, I think it shows, in a small way, how deeply the poem affected me, how much it made me think. I was young then, and responded to the calm optimism of the last few lines.

You could regard the poem as simply being "post-war"; written after two dreadful conflicts had shaken the world. You could, as Eliot did, think of it as a poem "of the atomic age", that period when, not long after, an even more dreadful, omnipotent threat appeared to hang over us all; this may well have been in the poet's mind. But now, it seems to me, if you disregard the references, early on, to conflict, you might consider it a poem of the "post-industrial age" and "post-carbon age"; when the products of the satanic mills which so haunted Muir, the pollution which was so casually dumped to foul the air and the water of this one planet which is our home, and the crazily-burgeoning human population with its endless demands on that planet, threaten our very existence. Is it crazy even to wonder if, given that grim and approaching scenario (of which there is now little room for doubt), that some vision for a human-scale, sustainable future could yet emerge in these quiet islands?

Twenty-four

Jean's War

At the outset of the Second World War, only twenty-one years after the first had finished, Donald John Munro called his three grandchildren, one boy and two girls, into his study and asked which of the services they would go into once they were of age. The question may have been rhetorical, I don't know; they all went into the Navy.

My mother, Jean, Joyce's only daughter, when she was old enough, applied to go into the WRNS, (always called "the Wrens", as it will be here), and to serve overseas. She was not exactly thrilled when "overseas" turned out to be Orkney, despite the fact that she knew and liked the islands, having visited Rousay with her parents in the 1930s.

But before that, she had had to go through the admissions procedure, some of which is well worth recounting. Much of the following is based on my mother's own written account, as well as some of her later reminiscences. I have occasionally provided some punctuation to help the reader cope with her fluent, if breathless, style – and there are a few names which I have not been able entirely to decipher.

> *"Eventually I was told to report to the Music Hall, George Street, (Edinburgh), for a WRNS Medical. I went along at the appointed time; after checking in, I was shown into a cubicle and told to strip, including shoes and glasses. When I emerged, I realised that we were all starkers except the many and varied medics. I was told to hold the back of a chair and jump on and off so many times, and then they sounded my*

heart. I was promptly told to lie down and calm down. The nurse said very loudly and crossly that she wasn't surprised, I had probably never been naked in front of a man before (she was quite right!). By this time I was trying not to laugh at the thought of the reaction of my father and mother to all this. When I got to the eye-man, he announced that I needed glasses! I said that I had them; when he heard that I had been told to leave them off, he went ballistic and stormed out."

In fact, by the time of her eye-test, my mother was getting used to the situation, and her irresistible sense of the ridiculous began to assert itself; she plucked up the courage to ask the man who was testing her eyes (which does involve quite close proximity, as most of us know), if he did not find it all a trifle distracting – there were about fifty girls there that morning, and he had examined them all!

"When we got outside, a group of us leant against the pillars, and wept with laughter; passing pedestrians obviously thought we were mad."

Because mother had attended the Atholl Crescent College of Domestic Science, the Navy decided she would be a cook, and after a fortnight's training at Balloch, near Loch Lomond, she found herself appointed to be Captain's cook, at HMS Sparrowhawk, Hatston, outside Kirkwall.

"At midnight I caught the Thurso train and spent the night on the luggage-rack in a carriage crammed with Navy, the sailors were always marvellous to the Wrens and looked after us as much as possible." Once at Scrabster, they "sailed into a fairly heavy sea; I stayed on deck with my gas-mask and tin hat, I didn't notice that the hat became detached and went overboard – a great start! An officer near me remarked that by the end of the war we would be able to walk to Orkney on all the tin hats."

Jean was to be cook to the Captain, Jeffery Gowland, who she liked immediately. His house "was an old farmhouse at the far or west end of the airfield, all the rest of the buildings were at the Kirkwall or east end. The back of the farmhouse was one side of the farm square, in the middle of which was a small building consisting of a bedroom with two bunks, a sitting room and a bathroom; this was where Peggy the Steward and I lived – very comfy, and out of the worst of the winds."

She had quite an exciting time at Hatston; "One day, I tried to take a short cut by climbing the gate to the main road. It was over six feet in height and covered with barbed wire. I got well and truly stuck and had to shout for help; who turned up but Captain G who roared with laughter and told me to get out of my skirt while no-one was about – which I did, and fled while he retrieved the skirt. I had to promise not to do that again."

"Another time when walking back from the camp along the runway in the dark, a man lunged at me. I hit him as hard as I could with the large rubber service torch which I carried; he fell and lay on the runway. I fled to the Captain and told him I thought I had killed a man. He looked at the torch and said he didn't think I could have, but phoned the main gate to go and investigate. Later he came and told me that they had found nothing. Next day a chap reported to Medics with a whacking bruise on his forehead and a very bruised shoulder, which he blamed on tripping and falling on concrete!"

"The job of Captain's cook was not difficult, and interesting; his guests were very varied (they included her father on one occasion), a lot of service people of course, but also folk like Yehudi Menuhin. I sat under the piano when he played in the crowded cinema; he was marvellous, playing anything he was asked."

After a spell of illness on board a hospital ship in the Flow, Jean returned to find that she had been transferred to work in the Officers' Galley. She enjoyed the greater company in the galley, but not the first Chief under whom she served. Fortunately, after a spell of leave, she returned to find that the hated Chief had been replaced by one much nicer, one CPO Lucy Fancy: "I couldn't think why I felt I should know her, so wrote to mother, who said that Lucy Fancy had been a cook at Auchindoune when my grandparents were there. When I said to her that I was Captain Munro's grand-daughter, she laughed and said, yes, that's who she thought I was, as I was very like him when I lost my temper!"

On at least one occasion, when the pressure was on, the Officers' Galley played its part in providing for the entire population of the base. Some big operation was being mounted, and there were thousands of men on the station; at one point my mother and one other were on their feet for over twenty-four hours, constantly cooking and serving, let alone dealing with the mountain of washing-up which resulted. In fact the wearing of wooden galley shoes irreparably damaged her feet; she suffered from fallen arches for the rest of her life.

> *"Looking back, I realise now that I caused Lucy and various older friends a lot of worry, as I was totally innocent. One night I accepted an invitation to go out in Kirkwall, with a stoker and a butcher. Consternation all round! I should not go, they were not 'the right sort', they were the sort that would put their hands inside your blouse (which I thought very odd!). I went, and thoroughly enjoyed the film, and the steak, egg and chips afterwards. I walked back hand in hand with them both, singing all the way — with a chaste kiss on the cheek at the Wrennery gate — Lucy and co were amazed! I went out with them separately and together after that. I also had a great friend, a Marine Driver always called*

Geordie (because, of course, he came from Newcastle!); he used to take
me with him when he could, I got all over Orkney Mainland that way."

She had friends among the Wrens, too. One came from Assynt, and
was the daughter of a family which Donald John had known and
with whom he stayed when occasionally fishing the Kirkaig – the
MacAskills. Mary, (whom I knew well in later years), had blazing red
hair, and was another girl with a temper to match. Apparently, my
mother was walking along the shore one day, when she wondered
what was causing the hullabaloo and the crowd of sailors and Wrens.
Somehow, it seemed, a trolley, with a live torpedo on it, had got out
of control, and for some reason unrecorded, there was red-headed
Mary MacAskill beside the torpedo, on the trolley, letting the world
know exactly what she thought of the situation and of the feeble
efforts of the assembled mob to regain control of it all!

"While in Orkney I met a Fleet Air Arm pilot, Raymond Mervyn
Mitchell. He was the son of the manager of one of the big coal mines in
Yorkshire – medium height, dark, definitely a bit wild. He once got me
smuggled into a Barracuda aircraft [the Fairey Barracuda torpedo-
and dive-bomber] *which I actually flew for about a minute – and*
nearly removed the Captain's chimneys! Why or how we got away with
it I still do not know. We got engaged, 'though my mother tried to ignore
it – and his father said, more sensibly, wait till the war is over. However,
his squadron was sent out east, then he changed squadrons (out there),
and I knew none of his new lot. He was never a good letter-writer...
eventually, through the grape-vine, I heard that he had crashed, and
the Japs had got him, and he was on the Railway... Not being next of
kin, and not knowing his home address, made it very difficult."

In fact, after the War, when my mother had still no clue whether

Raymond was alive or dead, and her parents seemed rather uninterested, another of her cousins (descended from Donald John's sister), who had connections in the Far East, took it upon himself to get Raymond's fate investigated. It transpired that he had, in fact, died, in the appalling conditions of the Death Railway. Despite the sad news, my mother was always grateful to Charles for his care and kindness when she was left in this state of limbo.

But my mother could provide comfort to others, too. Much later, when she and I were listening to a favourite Scottish soprano singing an Ave Maria (the one composed by Gounod, based on a work by Bach), she told me that she had sung it (she had an excellent voice, and, were it not for the War, might well have gone on to have it trained). She had learnt it at school under the cliffs of Salisbury Crags in Edinburgh (at the real St Trinnean's!), but had once sung it when in Orkney during the War. Things had been going badly, many planes during the day had gone out and not come back, all the boys presumed missing or dead. Most of the girls, of course, knew them, and that evening in the cold Nissen hut of the Wrennery, they were sitting alone on their bunks, most crying, all deeply upset. And then my mother began to sing. Why she chose this unlikely piece of music, with its Latin words, I have no idea, but her voice had real strength and beauty, and it rang out through that sad hut. When she reached the end, although the girls were still crying, they were together, their arms around each other, gathered around Jean.

I told that story, and we played that recording, on the lovely day when my mother was buried, next to my father, by the sea.

There were other tragedies, of course, and several much greater. One, the sinking of the Royal Oak by the little German submarine U-47 in 1939, is well-known, and the story needs no repetition here. Between the Wars, when the attempted salvaging of the sunk German Fleet was slowly progressing, easier targets came to hand. Much of my great-grandfather's boom defences was tidied away, "recycled" or plain lost, and one of the ships with which he had blocked the Kirk Sound was itself salvaged. It was through that gap, photographed by the Luftwaffe, that Gunther Prien made his audacious and successful bid, and gained fateful entry to the Flow. With what can only be called a tragic irony, the Admiralty were aware of this gap in the old defences, and another ship was at that time being towed north to fill it.

Donald John, then in (reluctant and active) retirement was called to the Admiralty to advise on the placing of solid causeways, the Churchill Barriers which we all know so well. To achieve the best line for this new venture, many of the block-ships were moved aside, off their original positions, where they remain today, still visible from the middle Barriers. No Orcadian today knows the name of Donald John Munro, but the block-ships and a small part of his boom defences (outside the Museum at Lyness) remain as a memorial to him. These, with the remains of the wartime airfields, the many gun emplacements, and observation points, are as much part of the long heritage of Orkney as the cairns and brochs.

He visited my mother once while she was at Hatston. They were talking idly over a meal, when he (who, rather like George Mackay Brown, was always conscious of his dual, Highland and Orcadian ancestry) asked my mother, most of whose life had in fact been spent in Edinburgh, where she felt she belonged – what was she? Without the slightest hesitation, almost to her surprise, she answered: "Orcadian". He appeared faintly amused, then looked out over the fields and the sea. "Aye", he said, "it gets you". My great-grandfather was no poet, but he got, quickly, to the facts: Orkney gets you.

Twenty-five

An Orkney Experience

I was born only four years after the end of the Second World War; it's the sort of perspective which is denied one in youth – as I grew up, the War was history, almost ancient history. And, of course, I was born at the mid-point of the twentieth century, an era whose first half had seen terrible conflicts, during which Orkney had been centre stage in the national struggle for survival. By the time I arrived in Orkney to live, thirty years later, all that had become a memory, the runways of abandoned airfields were dug up or grassing over, MOD buildings at places like Yesnaby demolished, crumbling or taken over by farmers. But there were some things to see then that have now disappeared, such as the Nether Button radio mast. To this day, however, plenty remains to remind us of the Wars, especially all the concrete gun- and observation-posts around the coast, the piers and other structures at Lyness, as well, obviously, as the Blockships, Barriers and exquisite Italian Chapel. Hatston still contains buildings which look like old hangars, and my mother and father, on one visit to us, spent an interesting hour or two exploring what is now an industrial estate, the scene of her wartime exploits.

When we arrived and settled in to the grey house on the Birsay Links, the very first thing to strike us was the warmth of the welcome from those who lived nearby. As we finished unloading the removal lorry which had brought all our possessions across a wintry Pentland Firth to a new life, our wonderful neighbour appeared at the door with a superb shepherd's pie. "You won't have had time to cook", she said, perhaps the most important words yet heard in the English language. Ruth and Tommy, and very soon many other folk in the little village of the Palace and nearby, became part of our daily lives, the cue for a wave or a chat on the way down to the little shop. When I had first arrived in the islands to look at the house where we would live, I knew exactly one person out of the entire Orcadian population, although I did know of some others. When, some years later, we decided it was time to seek pastures new, it was not because anything about life in Orkney had disappointed us, and most certainly not because we felt we had not made friends. The Orkney welcome then was strong, deep, and genuine, and we had enormous gratitude for that. I have been back every year since, and still feel that I am coming home.

My task in the summer season was to introduce people from elsewhere to the many and varied facets of Orkney, past and present, the places, sites and sightings, the topics which I have tried to describe in this book. As I hope will be obvious, the islands offered so much that I was soon deeply immersed in many aspects of their culture, and the constant questions of visitors helped me tackle some areas of ignorance, and organise the thoughts I had about what I knew. We, the three of us who constituted the Orkney Field and Arts Centre, worked non-stop during the season, one year for some twenty weeks without a complete day off – there is a lot to be said for youth! My wife organised the house and and did the cooking wonderfully, Florence from the village kept the public side of the centre immaculately clean, and I waited at table morning and night, while taking the groups around Orkney during the day. In five years, I only had to take two days off because of illness, and we probably only abandoned the outside world altogether, because of foul weather, once per season. It has to be admitted that if the Orkney weather makes up its mind to be really "coorse", it is impossible to withstand it – the only sensible thing to do is to stay indoors and read a book. We had, inevitably, the odd moment of stress and potential disaster, and, on occasion, resorted to the possibly rather dubious solution of saying to our two young girls: "Go and talk to the guests for a little while, we need ten minutes". Smiling enchantingly, off they went.

The moment when the last guests of the year had gone was indescribable; we used to make a lot of noise, use the whole house, I would wander naked from bedroom to bathroom, the cats and dog were allowed free rein. Soon we settled into the other part of the year, and our enjoyment of all the other aspects of Orkney of which we had been unable to take advantage because of our summer employment. For me, much of this was concerned with the lively music and art scene of the islands.

Because of the very discreetly located pipeline terminal on the Island of Flotta in Scapa Flow, Orkney Islands Council, which collected a royalty on every barrel of oil that passed through the archipelago, was a very wealthy Authority (as it still, to an extent, is). It spent a lot of money on education, including the provision of quite a number of peripatetic art and music teachers. These inevitably spent much of their leisure time making music with others, or developing their skills in the visual arts, and the result was a lively creative environment. Again, in these contexts, I was made very welcome, despite what I now see, all too clearly, as the immaturity both of my singing voice and artistic endeavours.

Despite my musical limitations, I ended up singing with the Kirkwall Amateur Operatic Society (which was enormous fun), with the St Magnus Festival Chorus, and, during Festival time, with the choir of St Magnus Cathedral. All this provided some very special moments and, on occasion, some tension, too. I remember singing in the cathedral, up on a high platform under the lofty crossing. Being one of the not very numerous tenors, I was in the back row, and in those days when health and safety culture did not dominate as it does now, was very conscious that I was poised, without a barrier, on the edge of what seemed like a very significant drop to the very hard-looking floor. One slight movement backwards would have seen us all disappear from view. The acoustics of the cathedral, because of its considerable height and narrowness, present the occasional problem; situated as we were under the crossing we could hear nothing of the sound we were producing, which we found extremely disconcerting. But I remember also an evening of late rehearsal just before the midsummer Festival, when we were still singing as the sun began to descend and send shafts of light through the great West Window. The shadows in the unlit nave, with its high red columns and pale vault, deepened from pink, to crimson, to deepest purple and a warm blue-black, and we fell, briefly, silent with wonder.

Peter Maxwell Davies, who very sadly has died while I have been writing this book, was a leading light in the Festival. On one occasion, I recall experiencing for the first time the intangible, but very real effect that a great conductor can have on his chorus and orchestra. It should be remembered that we were, largely, a chorus of amateurs. Despite the amount of instinctive musicality shown by so many folk in the Islands, and the presence of some professionals, we were struggling with the great complexities of Bernstein's Chichester Psalms – atonal, with bars of unequal length, singing in Hebrew, not precisely our comfort zone. In fact, most of us were extremely apprehensive, despite long hours of rehearsal. When it came to the day, Max appeared, smiled broadly at us, said a few words, and picked up the baton. We sang like angels, and none of us knew how it had happened.

On the occasion of my first trip to look at the Field Centre, something like chance had led me to call into an office in Broad Street, where I met a charming and very helpful man (sadly long dead, and much missed). Through his friendship, and that of his wonderful family, we rapidly got to know the members of two connected families in Kirkwall, all remarkably hospitable, and possessed both of good looks and musical talent. Most of them, it turned out, were in these various musical groups, and the very real fun and ensuing companionship made this, in retrospect, one of the most special periods of my life.

We also had good friends in Stromness (and a few elsewhere around the Islands); most of the former, but not all, were centred around the small congregation of the Scottish Episcopal Church which we attended. A visiting friend remarked once on the interesting contrast between the comparative formality of the wording and order of the actual services, and the warmth and informality of the congregation, led by the charismatic Minister. It was not unusual to see him, clad in his glorious vestments, halt his address to look down and smile at a toddler who had crawled up the church to him and was tugging at the fabric. If he had a fault, Michael was perhaps a little over-enthusiastic, a little long-winded. On one occasion, as he had entered the Church and we had all duly stood up, my second daughter, in clear, bell-like tones, turned to us and asked: "Why do we all stand up when Michael comes in?" As he reached his seat, Michael turned, smiled, said "That is a really interesting question," and proceeded to give us an impromptu ten-minute talk on the subject. Nothing daunted, he later gave us his sermon, of the usual length. You could feel the wives in the assembled congregation, all thinking of the Sunday lunch at home, beginning to be restless about halfway through.

Most of my artistic life was centred in Stromness, around the well-known Pier Arts Centre. We went to a number of exhibitions there. One of the most memorable was of work done by an artist from Aberdeen, Frances Walker, who had enjoyed an Arts Council Residency with us one summer. She was physically tough, and became quite a familiar sight in the village as she set off for the day, properly clad against whatever the day's weather might bring, carrying canvases and rucksack. Her total mastery of line enabled her to make sense of the complex beauty of the rocks and cliffs of the Buckquoy coast or the nearby Brough, and it was a superb exhibition.

In recent years, I have occasionally wondered quite how many Orcadians, as opposed to other visitors, go through the Pier Arts Centre, and I wonder whether it might not be an idea for it to aim to become the home, in addition to the exhibitions it already houses, of pictures of Orkney itself. Some would be by significant artists from elsewhere, like Frances, but there should, also, be an important collection of works by Orcadians such as Stanley Cursiter. One whose work should certainly feature in more than the two examples which I think are on display, is Sylvia Wishart, a friend and colleague (at Gray's School of Art) of Frances, and someone I so much wish I had met.

I have seen very few of Sylvia's pictures, and have had to rely on the study which the Pier Arts Centre itself produced. It is a handsome volume, although some of the illustrations are somewhat implacably gloomy. Sylvia, like Frances, had enormous technical skills, and she drew and painted many pictures of Orkney. The haunting valley of Rackwick was a constant subject; she and George Mackay Brown were alike in many things, and one was the inspiration they drew from the beauty of this (then) almost abandoned community. It was not all doom-and-gloom, though, the two of them would gather with other friends for the occasional weekend in which creative thinking was matched with good company and no shortage of food and drink.

I love the pictures of Rackwick, but it is the great series she painted of the view from her later home of Heathery Braes that really excites me. These are very complex pictures; the basic feature is the huge view out of the big window, which extends from the fields in front of the house, to that often turbulent patch of sea and the high cliffs of Hoy, with the Scottish coast sometimes visible in the background. There is often a foreground, the broad window-ledge with objects, a tea-tray perhaps, or a dish of fruit. In the fields, deep at times with standing crops, there may be a brown hare, or flying above, the unmistakeable short-eared owl. Closer to the shore, a flock of waders may be flying by, the ferry plying its way to or from Stromness, the sun setting or the moon overhead. And, as if this was not enough, in the glass of the window there are reflections: perhaps of things in the studio, perhaps a glimpse of the artist herself, pondering, looking out on the immense scene before her.

If you want to explore these pictures, or their deep implications, for the moment you have to buy the book: *Sylvia Wishart – A Study*. All I will say is that if I were rich, I would buy one, or as many of them as possible. I could spend quiet, content hours looking at each one of the series. I hope that one day a wealthy visionary may wake up to this great achievement of Orcadian culture, which I would rank with the Sagas, the Cathedral, Max's Orcadian music, George Mackay Brown's writings. I feel that such a collection would be a great asset to the Islands, and to the Pier Arts Centre itself – and of real interest to local people.

George himself I knew a little. We saw him often if we were in the Street in Stromness on a pleasant day. It is possible that I could have got to know him much better than I did, but a natural diffidence in the company of the great writer rather held me back from dropping in on him – perhaps quite wrongly. He visited us once, and stayed for a meal. I recall the scene clearly, George sitting at the table in our wood-panelled, stone-flagged living-room, the features, improbable but familiar from so many photographs, the wild hair, the blue eyes alight with mischief, the faintest scent of herrings, lively conversation with a real enjoyment of the presence of our young girls.

I was once asked to write a review of a small volume of his collected articles for the Orcadian, the column called "Under Brinkie's Brae". At first I found this rather intimidating, especially in the knowledge that I would inevitably see him not long after my review had appeared. But, of course, it was his writing that solved the problem for me. I decided that it should be treated like a Book of Hours, a Devotion, from which one might read each night, aloud, one small section, so that the magic of the prose, the careful selection of each word, the ritual world he constantly evoked, could be properly appreciated.

George wrote a great deal, and there are volumes of commentary on that achievement, as well as two profound biographies, and his own personal account of life: "For the Islands I sing". He created, out of the Orkney he knew and had read about, a fable, on a truly heroic scale, where the lives of the ordinary folk of the past (as well as the occasional Earl, Bishop or Saint), and the constant rituals of birth, procreation and death were played out against the passing of the years, set in the familiar landscapes of the Islands. Reading of his early life, his ill-health, his struggles with depression and the lure of alcohol, it would be easy to think of him as a timid man who rarely left home, but in his writing he could be outspoken, courageous, surprising. Of all that he wrote, I will offer one short passage from "Magnus", his account of the Saint whom he saw as central to the idea of Orkney, and his own creative life.

The sun climbed. In April the body of Magnus took a first kindling, blurrings of warmth and light. A slow flush went over his body.

The beasts in the field quenched their black flames, one on another.

The hill was opened by the plough. Fire and earth had their way with another. Was everywhere the loveliest spurting of seed and egg and spawn.

Girls fell into the rockpool, flowed, climbed out into the sun with sweet silver streaming bodies. They shrieked.

Magnus burned.

Twenty-six

Now and in the Future

Every now and again, there are national surveys to establish the best places in the country to live, and Orkney generally is close to the top of the list. In 2015, it was declared the best place in Scotland, but one or two of the reasons given, such as "the weather", (in 2015, the Orcadian summer just never happened – or, at least not until into September), failed to convince me. The provision of facilities, the quality of the education, the low unemployment, all sound much more understandable and convincing. But I felt, and feel, that the unsaid reasons are rather more important, and high on that list should simply be; the other Orcadians. Of course, generalisations are dangerous, and of course there must lurk somewhere the odd Orcadian who is bitter and twisted, but I never met one. I recall a few who could be a bit tedious, but with a little patience, and some avoiding-action, it was not too difficult to cope with them, and they were a real minority. Before, and since my time in Orkney, I have lived, happily, in many different places, but my memory of the Orcadians themselves remains special. The warmth, the friendship, the fun are what I remember most.

Some of this, I think, can be explained. There is a remoteness to Orkney itself, despite all modern communications, which engenders a feeling both of a mental self-sufficiency and inter-dependence, an unstated: "We are all in this together, and it is up to us to make it work". Social, or financial distinctions, which seem so significant elsewhere, are blurred. We all need each other to be there, at times. And because of the comparative remoteness, Orkney was never quite so desirable as a retirement area or place for a second home, in comparison with the Isle of Skye, or Assynt. This, and the comparative prosperity of the Islands meant that Orkney did not experience the same degree of distortion of the housing market, the feeling of being out-numbered by people from elsewhere, so there was less resentment of incomers. (I am aware that these pressures have increased to some degree in recent years, but it remains less of a problem in this archipelago than elsewhere.) Whether or not everyone in the Islands is conscious of their incomparable heritage of landscape and the endeavours of prehistory and history, there remains this very strong feeling of Orcadian identity, a positive bond between folk, with, mercifully, very little concomitant distrust or resentment of people from elsewhere. When I was living in Orkney, I knew a few people who had never travelled to the Scottish Mainland, or who had, perhaps, once gone to Thurso to see what the "Sooth" was like; you might think that such folk would be necessarily narrow-minded, truly parochial, but the simple truth was that they were content with being where they belonged.

The population of Orkney, at around twenty thousand, is not huge, and though you cannot know everyone, there is a fair chance that you will soon find friends in common. And the nature of that population counts, too; although the urban population is still growing at the expense of the outlying districts, there are several places where a genuinely viable rural population survives, where each house is within sight of others, but around which there is a bit of private space, places where the grass grows and the birds sing under a summer sky. The weather itself adds to the feeling of togetherness; everyone feels it, everyone rejoices in the light, and shares a sleepless night when the wind reaches a hundred miles an hour.

There is quite a tradition of strong individualism among the inhabitants of rural places, and Orkney is no exception, but it may be that some individualism is more happily tolerated than others. As I have hinted before, the impossibility of real privacy in Orkney must mean hardship for some, although the internet must greatly improve communication among some minorities. In a Scotland where, during my lifetime, compassion and respect for those who cannot conform to society's heterosexual norms is at last emerging, I hope that everyone can live a full life while at the same time being true to what they are, and feel no need to remain invisible. That needs to be as true for Orkney as for anywhere – in the name of our common humanity.

So much for the present; what of the future? And, especially, what of the future of Orkney as we approach, as we must, a future with far lower dependence on burning carbon? Orkney has succeeded in maintaining a fair degree of prosperity, but it has done so by establishing a successful import/export economy, whether we are talking of the export of jewellery and whisky, beef or shellfish, or the importing of tourists and the necessities of modern life, like foodstuffs or electrical goods from around the world. Increasing the value relative to weight of what you are importing or exporting can only be taken so far, and yet it is hard to see how local demand for Orkney's products could be stimulated enough to make comparative self-sufficiency, and the creation of a more autonomous economy, feasible.

I believe that Orkney has an enormous amount, quantifiable and unquantifiable, to tell and show the world, but that world is clearly changing, and Orkney does need to be prepared to learn from other communities as they adapt. Energy is obviously one field in which there is scope for growth, both in meeting local demand, and in exporting energy southwards. Renewables offer the chance to benefit from Orkney's physical location on the planet; its windy location has led to a considerable number of small-to-medium sized wind turbines, with just a few larger ones. I do not think that many visitors feel that island landscapes have been ruined by them, but there has to be some sort of policy on their location or, one day, people will wake up to the realisation that they have destroyed one of their most valuable assets, the quiet, fecund beauty of the countryside around them.

Orkney lacks the bigger landscapes of the Highlands where large pump-storage schemes work well, effectively storing hydro power. But the future must, in all logic, look towards the restless tides and currents which swirl around the islands. It must be possible, by careful study of the tides around the archipelago, to select locations where tides run at different times of day and night, where subsea turbines could supply much of the needed energy, all around the clock, filling in the "energy-gaps" when the wind neglects to blow. Of course, there would be problems to overcome, but the concept has a simple and undeniable logic to it, and we all, wherever we live, have to face up to the consequences of our own, seemingly endless demands for energy. Without readily available and genuinely cheap electricity, remote places, which have only just stopped being remote and disadvantaged, will once again retreat to the margins of the known world, and there remain.

It will take much cleverer brains than mine to plan a sustainable future for Orkney. The nearest community doing just that of which I am aware is the important Transition Black Isle, based on the peninsula just north of Inverness. The Black Isle is of the same geology as Orkney, and its low fertile ridges, if deprived of their trees, would remind you of Orkney. Although it is attached to the mainland, it has something of the island in more than just its name, and has an important marine history, based on its "noble harbour", the Cromarty Firth, where Donald John Munro perfected his crucial boom defences. The archipelago we call Orkney is composed, obviously, of islands, but the attitudes of its inhabitants could never be described as narrowly insular. That give-and-take with the rest of the world is more crucial now than perhaps it has ever been. Just as in the two World Wars, a great combined effort is needed – but it could achieve great things.

Twenty-seven

Family Footnotes

From Scapa, Donald John went on to Shetland and then to some of the sea-lochs of the West Coast, which the Grand Fleet had been using. At Loch Ewe, he met a young naval observer, Seton Gordon, who in later years was one of the first of the well-known Highland naturalists. By 1917, he was entirely confident of the effectiveness of the boom-defences he had installed in various places, and went on to other things. For a while he was Commodore of Convoys in the Mediterranean, and once again bombarded the Admiralty with suggestions for all kinds of practical improvement both in general practice and the precise detail of operating equipment. Later he was back on the South Coast, involved in all sorts of practical work, in which he clearly delighted.

He was made a Companion of the Order of St Michael and St George. The accompanying citation sounds to me rather dry, as it merely records his service in connection with the creation of boom defences, a rather minimal account of the invaluable service he had rendered to the operation of the British Navy in providing it with bases which were safe against submarine attack. Not that I am trying to mount a campaign for some greater, posthumous recognition, some higher honour. He has his memorial in Orkney, although his name is not attached to it, in the remains of the block-ships at Scapa, and the fragment of the wire boom defences that may be still seen at Lyness. It would be nice to think, however, that more Orcadians might become aware of the huge contribution he made to the safety of that great anchorage.

In that generation of the family, I must, however briefly, mention his younger brother, equally a son of Orkney, although it is not recorded that he ever spent much time there. Dr Hector Munro has been described in a number of books, because of his own remarkable characteristics. Clearly the radical of the family, he has been described as a "socialist and feminist", and a friend of both Ramsay MacDonald and George Bernard Shaw. He was also a vegetarian and believed in the benefits to health of naturism. Described often as a "pacifist", he was the sort of pacifist of whom any family could be proud, as he established a Flying Ambulance Corps operating at the front in Belgium. In this brave venture he employed many women, including Elsie Knocker and Mairi Gooden-Chisholm. Their extraordinary and very dangerous adventures are described in the book *Elsie and Mairi go to War,* by Diane Atkinson, which also sheds more light on Hector's remarkable character. After the war, he was influential in the founding of the Save the Children Fund.

Joyce remarried, and returned to Orkney on a number of occasions, the first of which was with her husband and daughter, staying at Trumland on Rousay with Walter Grant, a family friend; it was here that she acquired her interest in Scottish archaeology. She had to give up the piano and violin after serious neuritis, but developed her other artistic skills, which were considerable. She became a stalwart of the Scottish Women's Rural Institutes, The Handcraft Circle, and Embroiderers' Guild, travelling the country, demonstrating, lecturing, judging (and creating some truly beautiful heirlooms for the family). A couple of these trips took her to Orkney, and she went on a silver-smithing course there, too.

After the war, her daughter Jean (partly, I suspect, through sheer strength of character) got the job of Assistant Bursar at Hughes Hall, the Cambridge Teacher Training College. She must have been formidable; on discovering that the dons had butter (in these years of rationing) while the students made do with margarine, she cancelled the butter. She was known for singing at the top of her voice as she walked through Hall, and when faced with the task of running the College's PAYE system, sensibly acquired a boyfriend in the Inland Revenue. While visiting a friend in one of the men's colleges, she met a history student, one Bob Noble whose youth had been spent in the West Indies and Denmark (he was in fact half-Danish). She thought him the rudest man she had ever met, and six weeks later got engaged to him at Sheep's Green on the River Cam in the pouring rain. In some ways, it is perhaps no surprise that they ended up back in Scotland. He became a management trainee with whisky distillers John Haig and Company, ended up as Master Blender and Production Director, and eventually retired to Wester Ross. They had two sons, of whom I am the elder.

Jean and Bob visited Orkney at least a couple of times when we were living there, the last of those visits being for the family christening of their youngest grand-daughter, Sophie, who was born in Kirkwall. The christening was also attended by Joyce, who met, in the course of a wonderful service at St Mary's Church in Stromness, Lenore Brown who, characteristically, had befriended her on a previous visit to Orkney.

In later years, when I was working regularly in Orkney, my parents again visited the islands, and enjoyed, as I had done, the company and hospitality of a number of Orcadian cousins: Hugh and Erica Halcro Johnston, Jim Robertson, Margaret Watters and her niece, Anne Brundle. Jim, dapper with his neat moustache, dressed tidily in tweed jacket and flannels (how my father approved!), remembered Donald John, and thought him: "the eminent man of the family". My mother, talking to him, saw her grandfather's piercing blue eyes looking at her.

However little he may now be remembered, Donald John certainly left his mark on Orkney, and I hope I have shown, in brief, how Orkney left its mark on subsequent generations of the family, down to my two elder daughters, Mairi and Sunni, who enjoyed five happy years there. That Orkney has become part of my psyche, of my mental being is, I hope, also clear, and this book is my thanks to the islands and all contained therein, especially, of course, to the wonderful friends I made there.

But we always have a tendency, indeed we must always have a tendency, to think that there is meaning in our lives, that it all amounts to something, that family connections and old loyalties matter. In truth, it is all extraordinarily random, our being here the merest chance, and just occasionally some event proves the truth of this unpalatable fact. In our family history, we have one such event.

At Christmas time, 1915, being then still in Cromarty, my grandmother Joyce and her sister Sheila were invited on board ship to a seasonal film party. One of them was not feeling well, the weather was bad, and neither of them went. The ship was HMS Natal, and at three twenty-five in the afternoon, without warning, her magazines exploded, and within five minutes the Natal had capsized. It is thought that around four hundred folk died in that disaster. Had Joyce and her sister been on board, they would almost certainly have been among the dead, and they would, of course, have had no descendants.

Among my current, extended family, that means that there would be no (Scottish) Nobles, no Fentons, no Blanchards. Another branch descends from Donald John's sister, but their father, Charles, met his wife at a wedding which could never have taken place, so it is probable that none of those Munro-Faures would exist either. One small chance of fate, and all our lives would never have been.

Envoi

Sometimes I sense that visitors want the Orcadians to be more romantic in appearance, more "different". There is, sometimes, a hint of disappointment that many of them live in houses which could be placed anywhere from here to Cornwall, that most of them shop in Lidl and Tesco, that they watch television programmes on a Saturday night that everyone is watching all over Britain.

But living here is "different" in some ways. The everyday speech of the Islands may have lost much of its old Norn vocabulary (most of it is now simply Scots), but the accent itself, the intonation, is still distinct, still very Scandinavian, and, mercifully, shows no signs of declining. And a few aspects of life remain special, too, perhaps that bit wild. There is the collective anarchy of the famous Ba' games, played (if that really is the word), not for the benefit of tourists, but in the dead of winter when few of those are about. And there are the wedding parties, the groups going around on the back of a pick-up, horns going constantly, the groom (and sometimes, apparently, now the bride – separately, of course) blackened and perhaps already scantily dressed, only insulated from the cold by alcohol. He is likely to end up tied to the Cross in Broad Street, clad only in his pants, left there by his merry friends...

I used to bring groups to the Islands, and some of them would stay in a friendly country hotel (with superb food). The dining room and bar were together, and sometimes, when groups first gathered together on a Saturday night, the scene could be quite lively. On at least one occasion, such a wedding party did come in and the boys, including the blackened groom, gathered by the bar and got on with the serious business of the evening. I remember one woman in our group, who had been watching them closely, saying how nice it was to see a group of young folk clearly having a wonderful time, clearly well fuelled-up for the night, but behaving in an entirely inoffensive manner... and I quietly thanked my lucky stars that their Orcadian tongue was still so separate from everyday English to her ears that she had understood not one word of their conversation. They were farm boys, and their conversation was – fittingly, inevitably – earthy.

Later that night, I went briefly outside; the sky was not yet really dark, and I could see the outline of the big cliffs to the South. The lighthouse on the Brough winked at intervals, and I could hear the soft whisper of a breeze over the loch. The birds were still flying by, calling in the half-light. Briefly, a dog barked from a nearby farm, and then all again was peace.

Robin Noble

Acknowledgements

This book had been writing itself in my head for some years, and when it came to putting it on paper, it all seemed to happen fairly rapidly; I do not appear to have consulted many people about its content. That means, of course, that many of the opinions expressed within it, on a wide range of topics, are entirely my own and may be anathema to some of the relevant professionals. There are, of course, many books on Orkney and, where I have checked the occasional fact in one or other of them, I think that has been made completely clear in the text. I apologise sincerely for any omissions. I have to thank Dr Barbara Crawford for her helpful comments on matters concerning the complexities of the Earldom, which I found impossible to unravel on my own.

I am particularly grateful to Dr Anna Ritchie for reading my text, for her comments and advice, and for the Foreword which she has very kindly contributed. I also have enjoyed some helpful discussions and correspondence with Professor Jane Downes and Julie Gibson of Orkney College, UHI. As ever, Kirsty Macleod and Lesley McLaren have been devoted and helpful readers of my efforts and, in addition, Kirsty has ably kept under control the various bits-and-pieces which I sent to her at erratic intervals; most sincere thanks to you both, and to Martine Howard and Rhoderick Noble for their helpful comments.

I owe a lot, obviously, to those of my Orcadian relatives (all now deceased), who simply wrote things down while they remembered them – something we should all do! They were Margaret Watters, a fourth cousin and indefatigable genealogist, Donald John Munro, my great-grandfather, Joyce Menzies, my grandmother, and Jean Noble, my mother. My father, too, Robert Noble, collected and made sense of many of the family's stories. As a genealogist, he was ideal, being a natural sceptic, and a University-trained historian.

I have been so lucky in my Publisher; Sara Hunt has been kind and supportive throughout, and Craig Hillsley has equally been a pleasure to work with. Thanks too to Robbie Guillory, Ali Moore and the rest of the team, who work on such an interesting range of books.

Of course, the real stars of the book are the folk themselves of Orkney, so many of whom I have been proud to call friends. Many appear in the book, some by name, others without. I hope the latter will believe that nothing is implied by this perhaps apparent discrimination; in some cases, it just seemed too complicated to list everyone by name. The friendship of them all has been one of the most joyous aspects of my life.

And I owe a lot, too, to the numerous folk who have explored Orkney with me, groups from all over, from many sources, but most of all, perhaps, through The Travelling Naturalist and Aigas Field Centre. I thank them both for their support over the years, and, at Aigas, John and Lucy Lister-Kaye for their constant and unstinting hospitality. In recent years, a Ranger from Aigas has come on these trips, assisting generally, and driving, leaving me free to talk! Their company, too, has contributed to the relaxed enjoyment of these visits to these very special islands.

* The publisher would also like to thank Kathryn Haldane and Victoria Smith for their editorial assistance in proofreading and indexing.

Index

Author's Notes, Permissions and Credits

Wherever I have mentioned a location, a property or a walk, visitors should always check in advance for access details and whether it is safe or suitable for your fitness level. Visit Scotland will doubtless be glad to advise you. Please always respect the rights and privacy of those who live and work in Orkney.

I have referred occasionally in the text to the body that had, in my time, the overall responsibility for looking after the historic, built environment of Scotland, as "Historic Scotland". In 2015, Historic Scotland was amalgamated with the Royal Commission on the Ancient and Historic Monuments of Scotland, and the resulting body is called "Historic Environment Scotland". Where my topic concerns the current body, I have therefore referred to it under its new title. I hope the reader will not find this substitution, which is for the sake of accuracy, too clumsy or puzzling.

I have kept to what may be regarded as an old-fashioned form of dating: the use of "BC" and "AD". I find this still to be more generally understood by most readers than "BCE" and "CE".

The quote on page 16 is from a sonnet in *Collected Poems* by Robert Rendall, published by Steve Savage Publishers.

The quote on page 185 is from "The Horses" by Edwin Muir, published by Faber & Faber.

The quote on pages 201–2 is from *Magnus*, by George Mackay Brown, published by John Murray Press.

In the colour photographs section, all the landscape photographs are © Robin Noble, and all other photographs © Martine Howard.

The map opposite the foreword is © d-maps.com, available at http://d-maps.com/carte.php?num_car=15864&lang=en

Robin Noble

The Islands and Highlands of northern Scotland run deep in Robin Noble's blood. He is a naturalist who leads groups at the world-renowned Aigas Field Centre run by Sir John Lister-Kaye, and an eminent expert on the ancient woodlands of the Highlands. He's also an artist, singer and hill-walker. His history of the Highlands, *Castles in the Mist*, was shortlisted for the Saltire Society History Book of the Year award, whilst *North and West* explored Scotland's wilderness.

Anna Ritchie

Anna Ritchie is an archaeologist who has excavated Neolithic, Pictish and Viking-age sites in Orkney. Most recently she has been working on the early mediaeval stone carvings from Orkney and Shetland. Her books include *Prehistoric Orkney* (1995), *Exploring Scotland's Heritage: Orkney* (1996) and *On the fringe of Neolithic Europe: excavation of a chambered cairn, Holm of Papa Westray North, Orkney* (2009). She is a past president of the Society of Antiquaries of Scotland and trustee of National Museums Scotland and was made OBE in 1997 for services to archaeology.

Also by Robin Noble

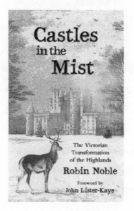

The magnificent Highlands of Scotland represent, in so many ways, ancient Britain. But much of this apparently wild environment is, in fact, far more recent in origin – it has been shaped by the Victorians.

Castles in the Mist reveals how, for better or for worse, the vast sporting estates of the Victorian era created the salmon rivers, deer forests and grouse moors, transforming the Highlands into the landscape that we recognise today, with its attendant environmental problems. In a seductive blend of autobiography, memoir, history and natural history, Robin Noble explores the colossal impact of the Victorian legacy in his beloved Highlands and issues a clarion call for change... to start tipping the balance back in nature's favour.

SHORTLISTED FOR A SALTIRE SOCIETY LITERARY AWARD